NO QUICK FIX (PLANNING)

NO QUICK FIX

(PLANNING)

Edited by
Frederic B. Vogel

Foundation for the Extension
and Development of the
American Professional Theatre

Frederic B. Vogel, Executive Director

165 West 46th Street, Suite 310
New York, NY 10036
212/869-9690

Library of Congress Catalog Number 85-070249

ISBN 0-9602942-5-2

$9.95

Designed by Joe Marc Freedman & Amy Shertzer

First Printing

Printed in the United States of America

CONTENTS

Frederic B. Vogel

PREFACE

When I assumed the Executive Directorship of FEDAPT in May of 1970, I envisioned offering a management technical assistance program with one long range goal in mind. Theatres would be allowed to fail *only* if they were artistically inept — not because of marketing problems, contributed and earned income shortfalls, board of trustees disinterest, box office inefficiency, or whatever else occurs to kill off a theatre company. While we are still a long way from fully realizing that state of Nirvana as this is being written in 1985, FEDAPT has been able to provide a wealth of information, guidance, counseling, and expertise to many, many theatre companies to help keep them operating long enough to reach and maintain whatever artistic potential they may have. Since 1979 we have provided similar services to dance companies, performing arts centers, and other kinds of arts organizations committed to strengthening their management structures.

FEDAPT's publications are a major component of the management services we offer. NO QUICK FIX (PLANNING), like all the FEDAPT publications that have preceded it, contains information that is vital to arts organizations' health and survival. The writers are working professionals who have, as consultants for FEDAPT and through other experiences, been involved in addressing the organizational issues that are crucial to us all.

One of the major reasons I went into Arts Management was that I felt it was highly creative. It was a profession which demanded the use of whatever wisdom, common sense, and judgment I possessed, and also demanded that I gather as much information as I could possibly accumulate in order to do a first class job. If you are of the same mind then you should look at NO QUICK FIX (PLANNING) as the source of the information you need to guide you through this organizational self-examination. All you will then need in addition to this book is commitment, concern, and a sense of excitement about the possibilities.

In certain ways, the four sections may seem repetitious. If so, be advised that this was a conscious choice on our part. Each section has been written by an individual whose style and sensibility differs from the others. This means that if you didn't quite see the entire picture through the eyes and words of one, you are surely going to understand more fully through the eyes and words of another.

Planning, like any other process or system has a jargon all its own which the writers herein have consciously eliminated for what we hope is greater clarity. We have, however, put a glossary of these words and phrases at the end of the book.

FEDAPT's Theatre Division Director Jessica L. Andrews and Dance Division Director Nello McDaniel have been extensively involved in the process of conceiving and writing this book. Quite simply, there would be nothing of sense to put between these covers without their contributions of wisdom, insight and knowledge.

On behalf of FEDAPT, I would also like to acknowledge the most valuable contributions by Robert Crawford, George Thorn, and Barbara Hauptman to this publication. I would also like to acknowledge the individuals listed below, who through their consultancies, their participation as seminar leaders, as speakers at our various workshops and conferences over the years have helped FEDAPT make this publication possible.

Robert Altman
Barbara Benisch
John H. Bos
Richard Bryant
James Clark
Peter Culman
Marcia DeGraff
Anne DesRosiers
Peter Donnelly
Douglas Eichten
Arlynn Fishbaugh
Marion Godfrey
Barry Grove

Alison Harris
Kenneth Hertz
Michalann Hobson
Karen Books Hopkins
Patricia Cox Hunchler
Gregory Kandel
Linda Kinsey
E. Timothy Langan
Baylor Landrum
Ruby Lerner
Michael Maso
Cynthia Mayeda
Joseph V. Melillo

Al Milano	*Simon Siegl*
Ben Mordecai	*Cassie Solomon*
Sara O'Connor	*Tom Spray*
John Ratté	*William Stewart*
M. Edgar Rosenblum	*Joel Stoesser*
Bill Rudman	*Carolyn Stolper*
Mitzi Sales	*David R. White*
Daniel Schay	*Robert Yesselman*
Ira Schlosser	*Charles Ziff*
Rena Shagan	

I would also like to acknowledge the creative editing efforts of Lance Olson, FEDAPT's Administrative Assistant.

FEDAPT would like to thank the Inter-Arts Program of the National Endowment for the Arts, the W. Alton Jones Foundation, The New York Community Trust, and the Xerox Foundation, as contributors to our Publications Revolving Fund for the period 1983–1985.

Robert W. Crawford

THE OVERALL STRUCTURE AND PROCESS OF PLANNING

WHY A PLAN?

There is no magic to planning. There should be no mystique about planning. Most individuals are involved in some sort of short-range or long-range planning in their everyday lives and don't really give a second thought to what they are doing. Writing a shopping list before

ROBERT CRAWFORD is a freelance consultant, working in all parts of the country with a wide range of not-for-profit organizations, private foundations and public sector agencies. In his volunteer work, Mr. Crawford has: served on the boards of eight not-for-profit institutions, including seven arts institutions; been a member of several National Endowment for the Arts panels, including six years as chair of its Theatre Advisory Panel; served as an elected member of the Vermont Council on the Arts and as a member of its performing arts panel. Mr. Crawford has authored a number of articles on the Middle East and compiled and written *In Art We Trust, The Board of Trustees in the Performing Arts,* published in 1981 by FEDAPT. In his consulting work with arts organizations, Mr. Crawford has worked principally in the areas of board/staff structures, relationships, and development; institutional planning and development; and fund raising.

going to the super market is an example of short-range planning. It is a listing of those items one knows one wants to purchase, based on the information at hand at a particular time. One may forget to include certain items on the shopping list, be reminded of the need for them when in the store, and then purchase them. Or one may find on getting to the store that a particular item is more costly than anticipated, or that it is out of stock. One doesn't purchase the item if it really is too expensive or if it is not available. Thus, based on a new reality, or a perception of a new reality, at some point later than the time the original shopping plan was made, the implementation of the original plan is changed. Often if an item on sale is not in stock, the store will provide the prospective buyer with a "rain check" enabling him to buy the item at the special price at a later date. This is a case of deferral of plan implementation which may or may not result in other alterations of the original plan to cover the interim period before full implementation is possible.

Thus, it is obvious that we are used to making plans in our every day lives, adapting them to changing circumstances over which we have no control. Or, as a result of new information or new experience, changing the original plan in the light of the new present. We don't think too much about making these changes because as human beings, we are likely to be willing to change the way or timing of getting what we want if we are convinced that what we want is worth getting, even at a somewhat later date than anticipated originally.

An example of longer range planning is planning ahead for a vacation. First, one must assess when is the best time in terms of one's work or family commitments to take a vacation. Then, if one intends going to a popular vacation area, one must reserve lodging well ahead of time. In order to get bargain rates for air travel, one must reserve and purchase tickets well in advance. Again, this type of longer range planning is accepted as a normal way of life if one is to be able to get where one wants to go at the time one wishes.

Buying a house, saving for the college education of one's children, or making a will are examples of long-range planning. In order to determine one's ability to assume a mortgage to finance the purchase of a home, one must assess not only one's current resources, but make a reasonable plan to implement the continued fiscal obligation for an extended number of years. If one has a family and if one assumes that each of the children may desire and be equipped to pursue post secondary education, and if one wishes to be in a position to help make this possible, plans for that eventuality must be made years in advance in order to determine how much of one's current income must be set aside each year for that purpose.

A particularly well accepted and understood type of long-range planning is the making of a will. In doing this, the individual plans, presumably years in advance, for the disposition of his assets upon his death. Wills are a good example of the flexibility of the planning process. When a will is written, it is usually well understood that it should be reviewed on a regular basis and rewritten as circumstances change. When it is written, it is composed on the basis of then-current information and then-current philosophies or concepts. As time passes, circumstances change, creating new information bases. To remain current and to reflect the then-current aspirations of the will preparer, the will (the plan) is reviewed from time to time and appropriate changes made.

The above simple examples of short-range, longer range, and long-range planning are cited to demonstrate that planning already is an integral part of virtually everyone's life. **Planning is, in reality, a common sense way of defining what it is that one wants, when one would like to attain it, and how one goes about attaining it.**

PRECONCEPTIONS ABOUT PLANNING

It is fascinating how difficult it often is for individuals to transfer their understanding of planning in their own lives, and its flexibility, to organizations of which they are a part. More often than not, when organizational planning is brought up or initially discussed, psychological blinders appear. It often is assumed that planning is a restrictive process; that the organization and its creative leadership will be locked into a plan which may well not be good for either; that a plan must be adhered to rigidly once it is formulated and approved; that change is impossible, or at the very best, difficult; that it forces people to do things when they realize from further experience that doing something else would be better; that because one doesn't know what is going to happen in the future, one is precluded by a plan from taking advantage of opportunities which may arise unexpectedly. To put it succinctly, such perceptions of planning are ridiculous.

Proper planning provides a truly freeing experience. It provides the opportunity to *dream programatically* and then to provide the most practical step by step implementation of those dreams. Planning provides the opportunity to use financial and human resources for the implementation of the purpose or purposes of the organization rather than having assumed perceptions of future financial and human resources dictate what can be done through programming. Planning provides the opportunity to work toward something rather than responding to *preconceived limitations.*

Some inhibitions to planning may well be a response to the very terms used in much organizational planning: e.g., strategic planning; long-range planning; objectives; goals; strategies. To the not-for-profit sector, the term "strategic planning" is probably one of the most inhibiting. To some, it conjures up a vision of the for-profit corporate mentality taking over the not-for-profit organization, limiting the creative leadership of an artistic director by forcing him into a perceived for-profit corporate planning mentality—the bottom line syndrome (profit or loss). It often is assumed that planning must start with financial planning and that programs are then created to fit budget preconceptions.

The concept that creativity is limited by planning is absolutely wrong. The successful dynamic for-profit corporation is led by an equally creative (entrepreneurial) individual or individuals as the successful dynamic not-for-profit corporation. The basic difference between the for-profit and the not-for-profit corporation is that the former, irrespective of its product or service, exists to provide some sort of return (gain) to those who own it, while the not-for-profit corporation is not owned by any one or by any group of persons, but provides its product or service to the public without providing any sort of monetary gain to any person or group from the income it generates through its activities. Normally, a for-profit organization which does not begin to show a profit after a certain period of time will not continue to exist. Individuals invest in a for-profit corporation in anticipation of receiving a monetary gain on that investment. Individuals do not "invest" in a not-for-profit organization as such. They contribute toward its program expenses in order to assure the availability and continuity of the products and/or services provided. They do not expect a direct tangible dollar return from this support. Rather, their return is the satisfaction of seeing something exist in which they believe either for themselves or for their extended community. There is no reason that a not-for-profit organization must lose money. While it does not exist to provide a dollar profit for any individual, the not-for-profit corporation certainly may end its fiscal year with a balanced budget or an excess of income over expenses. If this latter occurs, the excess does not get divided among any individuals, but is fed back into support of the product or service, or is used to establish a cash reserve fund to be available when cash flow problems might otherwise necessitate borrowing to meet current budget obligations.

THE POSITIVE APPROACH

Basic to any planning is a clear understanding of the very reason of the existence of the organization. In other words, what is its purpose, its mission. In the individual planning examples cited above in the introduction, the plan (shopping list) was to implement the purpose of obtaining food through the program (going to the store) of shopping. In another case, the purpose (to have funds available for later post secondary education) was planned for (an assessment of how much money would be necessary and when) and the program implementing the plan is the actual setting aside of the funds on the planned schedule.

A clear understanding and acceptance by all concerned (staff and board of trustees) of a not-for-profit organization as to what is the purpose — or multi purposes — of the organization must be established before any planning is done. The purpose or purposes, the reason for existence of an organization, is what justifies the utilization or expenditure of human and fiscal resources in activities or programs creating the product or service for which the organization exists. In order to be sure that there is consensus in regard to purpose, it is vital that each organization have a written statement of purpose, or mission statement. When filing for not-for-profit status, the Articles of Incorporation or Articles of Association must include a statement of purpose justifying the existence of the organization. This statement usually is a very broad based general one, frequently allowing virtually any sort of activity considered to be within the limits of the not-for-profit code of the particular State. For realistic planning, however, it is necessary to create a more focused statement of purpose.

For example, the Articles of Incorporation of a theatre company may state that it exists "to provide the highest quality theatre experience possible from all periods of dramatic literature to a widely diverse audience with attention to the interrelationships among the performing and visual arts fields." Such a statement of purpose justifies doing virtually anything and may well be appropriate in the Articles of Incorporation. But it gives absolutely no indication of any sense of focus and certainly is not conducive to specific planning.

Most organizations, however, seem to have some sort of assumed — if not clearly articulated or clearly understood — focus or artistic vision. The theatre cited above may be led by an artistic director whose personal commitment is primarily to the production of the classics, presented in repertory and through the use of a resident company. If this is the case, it is absolutely vital that the artistic staff, the management staff, and the board of trustees all understand clearly that this is the purpose. The implications of the implementation of such a purpose will be very different from that of a theatre whose purpose is primarily to produce an eclectic season of plays, presented one after the other, with casts selected specifically for each production. Mounting shows in repertory with casting made primarily from a resident company has significantly different fiscal as well as artistic implications.

Many dance organizations have had problems due to a lack of clarity of purpose. In recent years, the formerly rather sharp distinctions between the field of ballet and other dance styles have become much less clearly defined. If the purpose of the dance organization is primarily to mount and present dance in the balletic tradition, the statement of purpose should say so. If the primary focus is on the broad modern or post modern field, that should be expressed. If, and this is particularly applicable in the field of dance, the purpose of the organization is to provide the environment and opportunity for the work and further development of a particular choreographer, then the statement of purpose should state this.

In the performing arts there often is lack of understanding of purpose in connection with education or training. If a particular organization has as part of its purpose the pre-professional or professional training of performing artists then it should be included in the purpose statement. If the organization wants to educate its audiences or potential audiences by exposing them to the art form, it should be understood as one of the purposes of the organization. If there are any geographic or demographic components of the purpose, they should be stated.

Often, individuals become members of not-for-profit boards of trustees without really understanding the unique purpose or purposes of the organization, but assume that the organization is like their perception of other organizations in the same discipline. This problem is not limited to performing arts organizations. It is equally true for the entire range of not-for-profit organizations. If there is not clarity of purpose and a real understanding of it on the part of all, there are bound to be actual or potentially serious disagreements, particularly in regard to specific artistic/programmatic decisions and most particularly in regard to budget allocations. If the purpose of a dance company is to provide opportunity for and support to the work of a post modern choreographer, it is highly unlikely that the company will mount the "Nutcracker," even though some might think it would be a good fund raising activity. If a theatre exists primarily to encourage the work of new playwrights, it is unlikely that it will include a production of "Arsenic and Old Lace,"despite the box office draw it might have. If a music organization is committed primarily to the work of contemporary composers and librettists, it is unlikely to perform Beethoven or Verdi.

There is absolutely no right or wrong in terms of purpose. What is wrong is not to state clearly what the particular purpose is, be it very general, very specific, or a mix thereof. What is right is to be clear so that all involved with the implementation of the purpose, the staff and board, have a common base upon which to make implementation decisions. Such clarity of purpose also can alleviate many problems caused by fuzziness which frequently leads to ad hoc decision-making outside the framework of the very reason the organization exists. Over time, the whole purpose, or one of the purposes, may change. There is nothing wrong with this. But such changes should be dealt with consciously, in an up-front manner, rather than on an ad hoc, perhaps individual programmatic basis.

Programming is justified only if it serves in some way to further the purpose or purposes for which the organization exists. Over the years, donor institutions (private institutional and corporate foundations as well as the federal and state governments) have brought about changes in purpose in many not-for-profit organizations through the availability of grants for particular areas of program activity. Most private sector donor institutions have specific or limited general types of program which they are willing to support. Many search for programs or projects which are considered innovative and are willing to provide seed money or to provide limited years funding in order to get some new area of programming "established." Rarely do the institutional private sector donors provide ongoing or continuing support to that which they help get off the ground. With the unending search for new contributed dollars, not-for-profit organizations frequently tailor at least part of their programming to what they believe might be supportable from this donor sector, deviating in many cases from their basic purpose or mission in order to obtain the grant. The same is true with the public sector donors, although there has been a willingness by some public agencies to provide continuing operating support to organizations they deem worthy of support without such support having to be directed toward something specifically new and innovative.

The important point is that with a clear understanding of purpose, those associated with decision making and implementation in not-for-profit organizations can make sound decisions in regard to external support. If such support is in assistance of some part of the purpose, then it is valid to seek and accept it. If potential support is not keyed to the organization's purpose, then it should be rejected.

Assuming there is consensus on purpose, and that a clear purpose or mission statement has been prepared, normally on the initiative of the artistic and management leadership and approved by the board of trustees, planning can begin. There is absolutely no point in wasting time planning-to-plan. Some organizations trying to plan never get beyond the planning-to-plan stage as they get increasingly bogged down in what appear to be insurmountable complexities. What some think of as planning-to-plan is, in reality, part of the planning process itself.

What is needed for successful planning is conviction on the part of at least the artistic, management, and board leadership that planning is beneficial and vital to the organization's future, and a commitment to develop a plan within a specified period of time.

It should be agreed that the next fiscal year will be the first year of a multi-year plan, with the current fiscal year's programming serving as the base year from which the plan is developed. Throughout the planning process it is imperative to understand that the planning being done is based on the information and aspirations present at the time the plan is being made. Therefore, in a sense, the plan is out of date as soon as it is made. If this is clearly understood, it will help assure not only the necessity of regular review and adjustment, but the validity of doing so.

In order to be of value, a plan must be a "living" plan, reviewed at least once or twice during the course of each year and with a new year added to it just prior to the end of each current fiscal year. While the establishment or creation of the initial plan will take a lot of hard thoughtful work and consume a seemingly inordinate amount of time that might seem better used in other ways, once the plan is established its maintenance and revisions will take relatively little time. As a result of the plan, the more orderly development of the organization within the parameters of its clearly defined purpose will justify the original investment of time and energy. When completed, the plan will serve as the guideline for even more specific decisions to be made during the course of any given year, with modifications or changes being made on a more informed basis and made deliberately and consciously in relation to other areas of the plan, rather than on an ad hoc basis.

Among the many things provided by a carefully conceived plan is the opportunity to take better control over the future of the organization through the implementation of the planned use of human and financial resources. A plan provides the opportunity to make the best use of human and financial resources. It also provides opportunity to adjust realistically in the event of unexpected change in resources and to assess the impact of a particular program change on other components of the plan. In other words, it provides the vehicle to make rational considered decisions.

EXAMPLE: A theatre which had developed a five year plan and had been living with it and adjusting it for about three years, adding a fifth year each year, suddenly was faced with an unanticipated severe drop in contributed income. Surface logic seemed to indicate that the appropriate way to deal with this was to cancel the implementation of two new areas of program activity (increased artistic staff and a tour) and to reinstitute them in later years when there might be more funds available. Upon careful study of the plan and what the results of this action might be, however, it was determined that the effect of not introducing these programs during the year in question would, 1) have a serious negative effect on the overall development of the theatre and its role in its community, and 2) it could set back such developments by several years. It was decided, therefore, to maintain the introduction of these programs so that the momentum already generated in creating them could continue and to offset the reduction in funds by eliminating one of the mainstage productions. In addition, they trimmed a few other less major elements of the total operation. It was a traumatic experience for all involved and was a serious setback for that one year. It was agreed, however, that had there *not* been a plan which served as the point of departure for the discussions, ending with the decision finally taken, there might well have been very serious damage done by cutting out what at the moment of crisis might have seemed to be the most logical thing to terminate.

.　.　.

TO REPEAT: A plan serves as the guideline for making programmatic decisions leading toward a better or fuller implementation of the organization's purpose. It is an outline of how to get from where the organization currently is, to where it wants to go. It specifies the time frames, and what human and financial resources are necessary for full implementation. It is established at a given time and consequently is subject to constant review.

Having agreed that the upcoming fiscal year is to be year one of the plan, it must be decided how many years the plan will encompass. No matter what the scope of program activity, no matter what the magnitude of the budget, no matter what the size of the staff and the board, no matter how long the organization has been in existence, if it is assumed that it is to continue as an organization, planning for a specified period of time is absolutely vital to orderly, flexible development.

The first real planning that began in the not-for-profit arts sector in this country came as a result of the introduction of the challenge grant program by the National Endowment for the Arts in 1979. The Endowment decreed that in order to be eligible for consideration for a challenge grant, an applicant organization must submit a five year plan. Interestingly enough, the Endowment itself did not have a five year plan of its own, nor do many of the other public *and* private sector donor institutions which require plans of applicants. Nevertheless, the Endowment created the five year planning syndrome in the arts community. A number of at least semi-spurious plans were rapidly created in order to make organizations eligible for challenge grant consideration, but at least the lure of grant monies prompted the not-for-profit arts community to begin to look ahead.

Even for the most sophisticated of the arts organizations with multi-year track records, it is very difficult to plan realistically beyond three years. However, if it is possible to plan reasonably realistically for three years, it is well worth stretching toward five. Year four of the initial plan becomes year three very quickly. For newer organizations, usually of smaller budget and smaller staff, keeping going from month to month — much less year to year — seems often to be an almost overwhelmingly time consuming endeavor. But even organizations of this type, if they are ever to get out of their apparent crisis management attitude, should plan for at least a three year period. Again, year three of a plan very rapidly becomes year two. And in all instances, what an organization does in any given year has a definite effect on the subsequent year or years. Without a plan, it is difficult to see and understand these interrelationships, the effect any given decision has on decisions which will need to be made in subsequent years. If an organization has a clearly articulated purpose, if it is realised that the purpose or purposes are rarely fully attained at any given time, if it is accepted that programming is justified only if it serves the organization's purpose, and if it is understood that a plan serves as the guide toward attaining purpose through programming, then the necessity of looking at least three years ahead should be obvious.

Whether an organization chooses to make a three year plan or a five year plan, the process is the same. Assuming a clear definition of purpose, and assuming a commitment to developing either a three year or five year plan, the initial draft of the plan should be developed by the artistic leadership in concert with the management leadership and then be presented to the board of trustees, either through a planning committee of the board in the case of larger sized boards, or to the board sitting as a committee of the whole, wearing a planning committee "hat." It is vital in an arts organization that initial planning be done from an artistic, programmatic point of view keyed toward the best possible implementation of the organization's reason for existence — its purpose.

IMPLEMENTING THE PLANNING PROCESS

It is strongly recommended that in the preparation of a plan for an existing not-for-profit arts organization, the traditional strategic planning approach should not be followed.

Strategic planning focuses on how to implement programming, rather than on the creation and the content of programs. Such an approach tends to result in planning being done in terms of what seems to be fiscally possible, in the light of then-known resources or competition, rather than in terms of what the artistic leadership recommends doing to implement the organization's artistic purpose. Elements of strategic planning make sense later in the planning process, but if it is used as an approach to planning, it is almost sure to result in a great sense of frustration on the part of the artistic leadership.

Instead of following such a strategic planning approach, it is strongly recommended that planning should follow the fourteen specific stages outlined below.

STEP ONE: DECIDE "WHERE THE BUCK STOPS"

A formal decision is made by the board, in conjunction with the staff, that a plan should be made, when it should start, and how many years it will cover. Often, it will be necessary for the management leadership to take the initiative in getting agreement for creating a plan. Regardless of the origin of this initiative, the top management person should assume — or be given — the responsibility of seeing that the steps necessary to the creation of the plan are agreed to, a timetable is established, and follow-up is pursued. One individual must have this responsibility. That person is not responsible for creating the plan, but is responsible for seeing that it is done.

If there is reluctance, particularly on the part of board members, to pursue the creation of a plan, it probably would be helpful to have a special work session, or retreat, to bring the organization into focus through the process of self assessment. Normally, a session such as this demonstrates clearly the urgent necessity for planning. (See "Tools for the Planning Process," page 82, for a suggested ideal way of handling such a special work session or retreat).

STEP TWO: CREATE A STATEMENT OF PURPOSE

This should be drafted by the artistic leadership, reviewed carefully with the management leadership for full concurrence, and then presented to the board of trustees for discussion. If, as a result of this discussion, there are any differences or refinements needed, such changes should be redrafted by the artistic director, and resubmitted to the board for final formal approval. Board approval should be in the form of a formal board vote on the purpose statement. This action can help assure more active understanding on the part of the board.

STEP THREE: PROGRAM DEVELOPMENT AND SUPPORT CHART

The artistic leadership, normally in concert with the management leadership, should list vertically on the left hand side of a large spread sheet, every aspect of program activity taking place during the current fiscal year — the base year. Horizontally across the top of the paper as heads of columns should be listed the base year dates, plus the dates of the three or five years of the plan. This visual layout will make the finished plan clear and understandable. If desired, it can be supplemented later by appropriate narrative.

Under each main area of program activity (e.g., main stage productions for a theatre or home season performances for a dance company) the component parts of that program area should be listed. Among these might be:

- number of different productions
- number of performances for each production including whether evening or matinee
- type of production (classic, new play to the area, new play, comedy, musical, etc.)
- how many of each — the mix
- whether performed in repertory or back to back
- numbers in casts
- company basis or job-ins
- directed by whom — artistic director or visiting director
- staff or visiting set/costume/lighting designers
- locale of performance
- seating capacity per performance
- length of runs
- estimated number of paid seats to be filled
- estimated number of comp seats per performance/per production
- types of support staff (production, front of house, management) needed for each component, translated into some "common denominator" job description such as full-time equivalencies (FTE's), half-time jobs, seasonal, etc.

The above list of the components is suggestive, not definitive, and will be different for each organization.

STEP FOUR: DREAM A BIT

After listing all areas of program activity, one area should be dealt with at one time — totally separate, at first, from the others. If the plan is a three year plan, the separate areas of activity should be projected from the base year (the current fiscal year) to the third year of the plan, skipping the intervening years.

If, for example, the base year is fiscal year 1985/86, then the area of program under consideration should be described as it is now in 1985/86 and then as it is desired to be in fiscal year 1988/89, leaving the two intervening years blank. Then the planner should determine, from a strictly programmatic (artistic) point of view, how the change will be implemented in terms of program in 1986/87 and 1987/88, in order to get to the desired point of program activity in that program area in 1988/89.

The 1988/89 goal should not be established through the process of thinking year to year from the base year. Rather, it should be decided what the goal for each section of program will be for 1988/89, and then plan programmatically how to get there in the intervening years. In one area the 1988/89 goal may be attained in 1986/87, while in another, it may not be reached until 1988/89.

During this phase of the planning process, it is vital to handle each area of program activity separately from the others so that the full artistic or programmatic "druthers" can be established for each program area without the inhibition of relating one area to another and the resulting feeling that everything can't possibly be achieved, so "why dream." If each program area is planned separately and if full "druthers" are expressed, it is likely that the overall total programmatic/artistic profile of the organization for the third year of the plan (1988/89) will be more than the artistic leadership really wants to cope with. It is at this point and not before that the artistic planner should look at the 1988/89 profile as a whole, and determine from an artistic point of view what is most important to have achieved programmatically by that time, and then to make adjustments of the program goals for 1988/89 in terms of his view of the overall artistic implementation of the organization's purpose. In other words, the artistic leadership will at this point recommend the artistic priorities within and for the organization in terms of its purpose statement. This will then require adjusting what has been indicated as programming in the two intervening years.

Before this final adjustment is made programmatically, the artistic planner must determine if some activity should be taking place in 1988/89 which is not occurring during the base year. If it should, and it is placed in the 1988/89 column, it must then be determined at what point it should be introduced in order to be operative by the third year of the plan. Also, any planning activities necessary to the introduction of a new program area or support mechanism must be indicated on the plan chart in the appropriate time slot. It also should be determined if something being done in the base year should no longer be continued by the third year of the plan, or if there should be a downward shift in emphasis. If so, it must be determined when such a change will take place.

STEP FIVE: SHARE THE DREAM

When the artistic and management leadership have worked out the initial draft of the artistic program plan, they should present it to the board of trustees for discussion, or to the board through the Planning Committee. During this discussion, there should be *absolutely no mention of money* — that comes later. In the same way that money has not been a part of the initial steps taken by the artistic and management leadership, perceptions of cost should not inhibit the board from determining if they believe in what the artistic and management leadership is presenting to them from an artistic point of view, keyed to the best programmatic way of implementing the purpose. In order for this discussion to be productive, the draft of the plan should be circulated to all board members prior to the meeting at which it will be discussed, so that they will have full opportunity to study it before the discussion. During this discussion, the leader of the meeting must make sure that all understand fully the artistic implications of the plan and how it relates to the purpose. It is suggested that the chair of the Planning Committee lead this discussion. It also is imperative that the discussion not get side-tracked or bogged down with the potential fiscal implications of the plan.

What is needed from this discussion is a consensus that if funds were to be available to implement the plan, board and staff concur this is the thrust of program they all believe is best from an artistic/programmatic point of view. It is likely that out of the discussion some modifications will be suggested. If there is consensus on these modifications, then they should be incorporated by the artistic director in a revised version of the draft plan.

STEP SIX: WHAT ARE THE PRICE TAGS? WHAT CAN BE EARNED?

After consensus is reached on the artistic parameters of the plan, the artistic and management leadership then work together on the further fleshing out of the plan, including the fuller details of support staff and physical facilities necessary to its implementation. It is at this point that dollar figures are added.

In addition to estimating the dollar costs of implementing each year of the plan, staff also should estimate earned and contributed figures.

It is known what the dollar costs of implementing the base year are — that is the organization's current operating budget. In order to understand the real dollar implications of each year of the plan, each of the three projected years should be costed out in terms of the known base year dollars. It is easy to determine exactly what each of the years would cost to implement if it were being done in the base year. This is the reason for using base year dollars throughout.

For example, if a dance company is paying dancers on a per performance basis during the base year and is projecting a guaranteed forty weeks paid employment, at a certain amount per week, by the third year of the plan, it is logical to assume that there will be some sort of phasing in of this progression during the course of the three years. Using base year dollars for each year will indicate clearly what the annual budget implication of such changes will be and what will be necessary, given the base year knowledge and experience, to implement these changes through increased earned and/or contributed income. Of course, as each annual budget is prepared for a forthcoming fiscal year, that is the time that inflation factors must be added in — but not during the planning process.

The same process would be followed by a theatre company. If, for example, during the base year a theatre is operating on a "Letter of Agreement" with Actors' Equity Association (AEA) and plans to develop into a "LORT D" company by at least the third year of the plan (or if it is moving from a "LORT D" contract to a "LORT B"), it is easy to determine what that would cost if it were being implemented during the base year. Those are the dollar figures which should be used in the plan. No one knows at the moment of planning what the AEA agreements will call for in terms of salary minimums three years in the future, but when subsequent annual budgets are prepared, those changes can be entered into the budget in the same way other inflationary factors or escalations are handled.

STEP SEVEN: SHAKE DOWN THE BUDGET

When the artistic and management leadership have completed their work on the fiscal aspects and other fleshing out of the artistic plan, it should be reviewed in careful detail with both the Finance and Fund Raising Committees of the board. It is suggested that these be separate discussions rather than having the committees meet in joint session.

There is a different psychological approach when looking at a budget from a finance committee member point of view and from a fund raising committee member point of view. These discussions, probably pretty "scary" at first, should focus on the validity of the expense and earned income figures by the finance committee, and the varied sources of contributed income needs by the fund raising committee. The discussions should not get bogged down by perhaps emotionally based assumptions that because of past experience, an increase in contributed or earned income is impossible. Rather, focus should be initially on the validity of the figures and identification of the areas of new earned and contributed income necessary to implement the plan, the artistic part of which already has been agreed to in principle by the board and the staff. The results of these discussions should then be reported to and discussed by the Planning Committee.

STEP EIGHT: SET PARAMETERS

Having determined what the magnitude of each annual budget will be in terms of base year dollars to implement the proposed plan, it should be agreed that this becomes known as Plan A. The fiscal parameters for a Plan B and a Plan C should then be established by a joint session of the Finance, Fund Raising, and Planning Committees. For example, if Plan A calls for an annual operating budget in the third year of the plan of $1 million in base year dollars, and if the base year budget amounts in fact to $500,000, the joint meeting (with staff included of course) might conclude that the third year budget should not be more than either $800,000 (Plan B) or $675,000 (Plan C). This joint committee *should not suggest what the programmatic content of Plan B or Plan C should be,* but should direct the staff to return with their program recommendations based on those alternate base year dollar budget limits.

STEP NINE: DEVELOP OPTIONS (BEST TO WORST)

At this point, the artistic and management leadership work together again revising the third year of the plan from a programmatic point of view to achieve the program best suited to the purpose of the organization by that year within the suggested financial constraints. Having done this, they then revise the intervening two years between the base year and the third year of the plan. In doing this, they will end up with three plans showing the rate of implementing the artistic priorities within the constraints of three separate dollar totals: Plan A will be what is really wanted; Plan B will be what is really possibly attainable with the concentrated effort of all; and Plan C will be a minimum of what must be done. An advantage of proceeding in this manner is that there is, as a result, very specific rational justification for seeking funds keyed to Plan A even though the Plan B budget may be the internally approved budget. If such additional funds are in fact acquired, elements of Plan A can become an implementable part of Plan B.

STEP TEN: COMMITTEE REVIEW

The artistic and management leadership present the revised plans A, B, and C to a joint meeting of the Finance, Fund Raising, and Planning Committees for their review and any further comments.

STEP ELEVEN: FULL BOARD REVIEW AND CONSENSUS

The plan is then presented by the Planning Committee to the board as a whole. Again, the draft document should be sent out ahead to all board members so there is time to study it in advance of the meeting. At this meeting, the artistic director should verbalize the artistic plan, the management leadership should verbalize the administrative and support aspects of the plan, the chair of the Finance Committee should verbalize the process of the budget development, and the chair of the Fund Raising Committee should verbalize the fund raising implications. The chair of the Planning Committee should moderate and facilitate the overall discussions and presentations.

Each presenter should share with the board how certain recommended decisions were arrived at (e.g., the pros and cons if there were differences and how they were resolved) and board members not serving on those committees should be encouraged to raise questions. By the end of this meeting, there hopefully should be a high degree of consensus, but no formal vote should be taken.

STEP TWELVE: THE REDRAFT

Based on the discussions with the full board, the artistic and management leadership in further consultation with appropriate committee members if necessary, should make a final revision of plans A, B, and C and distribute them to all members of the board through the chair of the Planning Committee.

STEP THIRTEEN: VOTE ON THE PLAN

The plan should be discussed in its final form at a special meeting of the board and should be acted upon by formal vote of the board. While Plan A will presumably become the acknowledged publicized plan, it should be determined internally which plan is most likely to be implemented through the combined efforts of board and staff. Presumably Plan C would be be considered as a fall back position plan, not what is wanted.

STEP FOURTEEN: THE CARE AND FEEDING OF THE PLAN

Once the plan is established it must be kept alive. At least once during the course of the fiscal year, approximately the middle of the year, the plan should be reviewed by the artistic and management leadership with the Planning Committee and a report made to the full board. This review should determine how much is actually being accomplished and what is not. Initial adjustments to the forward part of the plan should be made at this time. Further, by the end of each fiscal year a new year must be added to the plan. The process of adding this new year will follow the same steps as in the creation of the original plan, but should require comparatively little time.

A CONTEXT FOR CHANGE

Creating a three or five year plan may seem a perhaps onerous task. It is not. It deals with the implementation in an ordered way of the very reason for existence of the arts organization. If the plan is maintained and kept alive, it will provide a context within which to make flexible and creative program decisions and will allow change and the introduction of new concepts or programs not originally thought about at the time the plan was made.

Each new idea or proposed change will be measured against what was determined at an earlier date to be best for the organization. In the light of further experience and new information and ideas, some of that which was originally planned might be inappropriate or out of date. By using the plan as a point of departure, changes will be made in a considered sense, in terms of the whole, rather than on a perhaps ad hoc basis.

The plan serves as a guide line or road map. It also is an enormous asset in raising contributed income. The plan demonstrates that each contributed dollar is going to be used to get somewhere rather than just in support of a year to year ad hoc type of operation. Finally, rather than allowing perceived possibly limited resources to dictate where an organization should go, a plan enables an organization to better control its own destiny, to use its financial and human resources in support of something to which it aspires.

George W. Thorn

STEP BY STEP PROCEDURES ▪ A PRACTICAL APPROACH TO PLANNING

EFFECTIVE PLANNING: THE CAST OF CHARACTERS

THE ORGANIZATIONAL (THREE-WAY) PARTNERSHIP

An arts organization is a working partnership of artistic leadership, board leadership, and management leadership. There are the realities of employer and employee, organizational charts, and titles, but the working, functioning reality must be one of partnership.

GEORGE THORN divides his time between being an arts management consultant and directing the graduate program in arts management at Virginia Tech in Blacksburg, Virginia. Prior to these activities he was the fiscal and administrative officer of the Eugene O'Neill Memorial Theater Center. Mr. Thorn spent sixteen years in New York where his general management firm managed Broadway, Off-Broadway and touring productions. Mr. Thorn serves as a consultant to FEDAPT theatre and dance companies and has served as the Co-Director of the Regional Theatre Management Technical Assistance Program with the Pennsylvania Council on the Arts. He has also served as the Co-Director of FEDAPT's Theatre Workshop Program for Organizational Development in Minneapolis– St. Paul.

Each component has its own duties, obligations, responsibilities, and structure. It has its own job to do and its own sphere of influence. These three spheres are totally inter-connected and inter-dependent. One cannot act or succeed without the other two fulfilling their responsibilities.

Strong artistic and board components with weak management will cause some problems. A strong artistic and management team with a weak board will cause some problems. A strong board and management with a weak artistic component, and their may be no hope for the organization.

This three-way partnership meets at a common center which must be the artistic vision and mission of the organization. The partnership could be graphically represented as follows:

THE ORGANIZATIONAL (THREE-WAY) PARTNERSHIP

PLANNING IS A KEY *OPERATIONAL* ELEMENT

Planning must involve the whole organization, and evaluating the effectiveness of the plan must be an ongoing and active part of the organization's operations. Too often, planning has been seen as a way to get a prize, and not as an organizational necessity.

Planning should not be solely the province of a long-range planning committee, or the staff. A plan developed by a small group and merely adopted by the organization will likely find itself on the shelf gathering dust shortly after its adoption. If, on the other hand, development of the plan is an activity of the total organization, then artist/board/management will share in the ownership of the plan and will use it as an active and dynamic guide for operation and evaluation. The plan will then serve as the common frame of reference for all decision-making by all levels and components of the organization.

THE BENEFITS OF PLANNING

Developing a long-range plan requires a sizable commitment from everyone; it is, however, a necessity. The planning process can be useful in guiding all facets of the organization toward the same goals. Particularly with new, emerging organizations or those in transition, the process of developing the plan will focus and direct everyone's energies in a positive and creative manner.

The completed plan must be regarded as an organic and dynamic course of action for operation, growth, and development. It should not, however, be viewed as chiseled in stone or set in concrete. Nor should the plan be placed in a drawer and forgotten. It is a flexible, working guide. The plan serves to liberate the organization by harnessing and focusing all its energies toward achieving success.

We must not forget or overlook the fact that planning, operation, and evaluation are ongoing and always connected. The planning committees are also the operational committees. Operation and planning can only be effective with complete and thorough evaluation. The plan is the benchmark, the point of reference for all decisions. All choices are made in keeping with the plan or as a conscious decision to alter or change the plan.

The completed plan may also be utilized as the basis for the development of an organizational prospectus. The prospectus would include the positioning statement, brief history, a summary of the plan, list of the board of trustees, brief resumes of the senior staff, the specific needs of the organization, and the ways in which people can involve themselves with the organization.

The prospectus, the plan and the annual report will serve as invaluable tools in organizational image building, marketing, fund raising, board recruiting, and publicity. These documents need not be expensive, but must truly reflect the organizational style and look. An imaginatively-designed and well-printed prospectus and annual report are worth the investment of time and money.

FRAMES FOR PLANNING

For an organization to operate effectively, it must have a defined, articulated, understood and agreed upon vision/mission/purpose. This holds true for every aspect and every function of the entire organization. And this vision/mission/purpose must be firmly in place before the planning process can be initiated.

The mission of an organization can be thought of as a frame described by a particular structural shape. Metaphorically, is the organization a triangle, square, circle, or trapezoid?

Once it is agreed that the frame is (for example) a triangle then everyone has his/her* job to do in filling in the particular frame. All resources and energies are focused on the same goals and priorities.

Persons not agreeing with the mission, goals, and priorities should not continue with the organization. This does not mean there will be "Rubber Stamp" unanimity—far from it—but the growth and development of a not-for-profit arts organization is an extremely fragile undertaking. There is no room for devil's advocates or diffusion of energies. Rather, there must be support for the goals with unqualified work and energy.

With the frame in place, it is possible to begin the planning process.

GETTING UNDERWAY

WHO'S IN CHARGE?

The responsibility for initiating, managing, and directing the planning process ultimately rests with the artistic director, the managing director, and the president or chair of the board. These three will constitute the underlying energy and force necessary to achieve the goal of completing the plan, though the board committees will ultimately

---

* The author has requested the use of the personal pronoun form "he/she" in this section of the book.

have to be challenged and directed by the president. Staff cannot lead the board through the planning process, though these individuals will have the responsibility for most of the basic research, writing, and providing support materials and information to the committees.

A problem will arise if the president or chair of the board is not an effective leader or is not supportive of the planning process. One possible solution to such a situation is to maneuver the president into appointing a chair of the long-range planning process and having the board create a long-range committee made up of the chairs of the board committees, complemented with the artistic and managing directors. The appointment of a positive and forceful leader as the chair of the committee is essential. The president must also clearly charge the group with the responsibility and authority to investigate all areas of the organization and complete the plan.

THE CYCLES OF PLANNING

A fundamental in the planning cycle is the organization's decision on how many years the plan will cover. This is a decision that will be made by each organization depending on its present situation and needs. A five-year planning cycle is strongly recommended.

The first time an organization undertakes the development of a long-range plan, it usually tends to opt for a shorter time period — three years, for example. This decision is generally the result of resistance to developing a plan in the first place. "We don't know where we'll be next week — how do we know where we'll be in three years"; "A plan will be restrictive, box us in — we want to keep our options open." These fears, however, are mistakenly and naively engendered, since any plan worth its salt will be reviewed and evaluated at the end of each year, altered to reflect new information and changes in the organization's environment, and extended for another year.

THE MYTH OF THE SHORT TERM

Although five years may seem a long time for an organization, the first year in most cases is already in place. Even if there has never been a long-range plan, every organization has (whether it knows it or not) a short-term plan for its next year. Decisions will have been made on such matters as season, budget, marketing (at least a renewal subscription campaign), grant writing, and annual giving campaign. Regardless of how detailed these decisions are, at a minimum they do constitute a kind of short-term plan, and form the basis for a five-year plan.

Actually, the notion that short-term, one-year plans can exist is a figment. The reality is that the short-term planning cycle in today's environment must be at least for two future years, combined with the operational plan and budget for the present year. Foundation (public and private) grant deadlines and corporate funding cycles are just two of the reasons for this required two to three years of "short-term" planning.

Most arts organizations assemble a series of project-to-project budgets and grant narratives to meet these various deadlines. Then, as the organization approaches the next operational year, it assumes these project grants as a given and incorporates them as a part of the operational plan.

It is much more prudent and effective for an organization to have ready a one-year draft plan and budget and a sketch of a second-year plan and budget. Then, as needs arise (for example, to execute grant proposals), one pulls out of the existing plan and budgets the appropriate information for the proposal.

An organization operating without an approved plan or budget provides an example of the absence of even a short-term plan. Even worse are organizations with a budget that purports to be a plan. A budget is not a plan. A budget is a series of price tags for the organization's functions.

The two-year, short-term plan, plus the present operational plan, serve as the basis for developing plans for years three, four, and five.

YESTERDAY, TODAY, AND TOMORROW

The process of planning begins with the partners understanding and agreeing upon three points:

1. the evolution of the organization;
2. the present status of the organization;
3. the artistic vision for the organization over the next five years.

In other words, where did we come from and where are we now? Where and what will the organization be at the end of the fifth year? What is the esthetic center of the organization, and how will that esthetic be realized in the work created by the artists? What will it look like, and what will its programs be?

The artistic leadership initiates this discussion, presenting its ideas to the other partners and helping them understand this vision for the next five years. The artistic leadership of a professional arts organization is its artistic or producing director(s). In a *totally* volunteer organization, this vision of the organization may have to be developed by the board functioning as a committee of the whole.

CREATIVE FACE, PUBLIC FACE

One approach to developing this presentation is for the artistic leadership to articulate the esthetic, philosophical center of energy and the two faces of each organization: the "creative face" and the "public face."

The creative face is constituted of the process of creating the work for which the organization exists:

1. Style, form, content of the work.
   a. Dance — classical ballet, modern, post-modern, repertory company, focus on the work of a single choreographer, etc.
   b. Theatre — new playwrights, Shakespeare festival, classical, musical, eclectic, etc.
2. Seasons — Mainstage, second stage, home seasons, specials, *Nutcracker*, *Christmas Carol*, touring, etc.
3. Amount of work to be originated by artistic leadership.
4. Number of performers — resident company, jobbed in, or pick-up.
5. Quality of artists.
6. Guest artists — choreographers, directors, designers, writers, composers, etc.
7. Production values, scale, and size.
8. Artistic staff — dramaturge, ballet master/mistress, associate director, school director, designers, production support, etc.
9. Touring — amount, performance opportunities, etc.
10. Length of rehearsals.
11. Educational outreach programs — lecture demos, touring to schools, etc.
12. School — style, professional training, avocational, teachers, curriculum, location, studio, etc.

13. Facility—performance, rehearsal, shop spaces, offices, school studios, storage, etc.

14. Presenting other companies or other arts disciplines, exhibit space, other dance forms, chamber music, etc.

The public face is how the work is shared with the organization's constituencies:

1. Length of run of each performance activity.

2. Number of performances.

3. Series or special events.

4. Touring.

5. Outreach

6. School

7. Classes

8. Facilities

This part of the presentation parallels the creative face by addressing how the audience or communities will be exposed to, and served by, the work.

PRESENTING THE DREAM

In preparing this presentation of the artistic vision, it is necessary for the artistic leadership to *forget* time, space, and money. This is the time to *dream* about what the work and the organization should be at the end of the fifth year. We must not be concerned with *how* these goals will be accomplished—that is the purpose of the subsequent plan. However, it is essential that the order of priority and sequence be a part of this presentation.

When completed, this five-year projection of the organization's artistic vision (the 14 points enumerated under creative and public faces) should be presented in its entirety to the board and management leadership together so that everyone has a sense of the scope and scale of the vision and direction. It will then be necessary to work through the presentation area by area until complete understanding and agreement are reached.

As much time as is necessary should be taken for full, open discussions to ensure *both understanding* and *agreement*. Every act, decision, budget, promotion campaign, and image will flow from this agreement on vision and direction.

WHAT IS SUCCESS?

A basic human drive is to want to know how we are doing. Are we successful, did we meet our goals? Internally, the organization is constantly asking itself these questions. Externally, funding agencies, media, and sponsors are always applying their own assessments of the organization's success. Defining success is the next hurdle after identifying the artistic vision.

The criteria for measuring success must be developed for each organization's unique vision — its place in the arts discipline and its position in the community. They will vary from organization to organization and from art form to art form.

Arts organizations should not see themselves in competition with other organizations working in the same discipline, nor in competition with other disciplines. An arts organization is, in reality, in competition with itself. Did we do what we said we would do at the level of quality we set for ourselves? Did we do it when we said we would? Were we successful on our own terms? Each organization must understand and agree on these measurements internally and then communicate this understanding externally so that everyone else is judging its success in an appropriate manner.

An excellent example of defining the criteria for measurement of success and communicating that criteria to the world at large is the implantation of the second artificial heart.

Prior to the operation, the surgeon said the operation would be a success if the patient had one day of life with a better quality than he had the day before the operation. *Implied* is that even if the patient's life was not extended significantly, the operation would still have been successful.

The world was also informed that the operation would be successful if simply by doing the operation they would know more than they would by not having performed the operation. *Implied* is that even if the patient died during the procedure, the operation would be successful. The surgeon told us they were committed to doing a hundred of these procedures and that each would be successful because they would learn more from each one they did.

The widow of the recipient of the first implant stated her late husband's operation was a success because what had been learned from that process would aid this second implant. The doctor who developed the artificial heart said that the life expectancy of the pump is three to five years. *Implied* is that even if this operation is successful by all criteria, the entire procedure will need to be repeated again in three to five years. And so on . . . .

Each organization must be as precise and clear in understanding, agreeing upon, and communicating its own criteria for measurement of success.

THE "MARKETING EXECUTIVE" PITFALL

In measuring success, it is important to understand one of the basic differences between the for-profit and not-for-profit organization. In the for-profit sector, a product is created or altered to meet a perceived consumer need. Also, there is the money to research and survey to determine if the perception of need is a reality. If not, the money and research are available to convince consumers that they have an undiscovered need.

In a not-for-profit arts organization, our product is given to us by our artists. It is then up to everyone in the organization to lead the consumers to that product. This premise is based on the following assumptions:

1. the artist is a part of the community in which the organization exists;

2. the artistic product is only realized when shared with an audience;

3. the artist understands the balance between responding to and leading the audience.

It is unrealistic to believe that a lasting audience can be built by giving it what we think it wants and then turning 180 degrees and programming something else, even if it is good art we really want to do. The audience will feel hoodwinked or confused and it will seek to fulfill its desires elsewhere.

COMPARE CAUTIOUSLY

It is destructive, either internally or externally, to see the larger, more established arts organization as the artistic and structural model that everyone should follow. We must not judge ourselves in relationship to another organization, but should develop evaluative criteria that are unique and appropriate for our efforts and structure.

THE STATISTICAL ANALYSIS TRAP

There are, of course, some general arts-wide statistical criteria that are usually employed in evaluating arts organizations:

1. Balance or imbalance of budget

2. Ratio of earned to contributed income

3. Size of budget

4. Number of subscribers

5. Cash reserve

6. Size of deficit, shortfall, or surplus

7. Critical response

8. This season's percentage of seating capacity

9. Rate of growth

10. Who is on the Board of Trustees

These are all valid measurements of success. But each one must be used in the context of the vision and type of work. And, in some cases, they might prove totally invalid.

Ratio of earned to contributed income certainly varies greatly from discipline to discipline and will vary greatly within an art form. A theatre which produces only new plays, in contrast to a theatre that produces a wide-ranging repertory including two musicals, will have dramatically different ratios of earned to contributed income.

For the wide ranging repertory theatre, it may be very appropriate (indeed, vital) to have a large subscription base. For a new playwrights' theatre that only produces a play when the script is deemed ready for public viewing (hence, obviating the possibility of advertising a "season"), a small or no subscription-base might be appropriate. However, if both theatres are meeting their goals, both are successful in fulfilling their respective missions.

A classical ballet company that includes *Nutcracker* as a special event and a contemporary dance company devoted to the works of its artistic director may have a much different ratio of earned to contributed income.

Let us look at some of the examples of misunderstanding of measurements that are often applied:

1. A modern repertory dance company in a mid-size midwestern city is playing 10 performances to a half-filled house; it has a small subscription base. The leadership questions itself because performances are not sold out. In this case, the leadership needs to recognize not only that it will take time to build an audience, but that a certain number of performnaces are essential for the dancers to have the performance opportunities to develop their repertoire.

2. "All dance companies tour. All touring makes money. If we toured, we wouldn't have to raise as much money." Touring is not necessarily a profit center. Touring needs to be seen as creating performance opportunities to develop the work and visibility. Touring requires a major investment in booking and management. Touring is very stressful for the dancers and takes time away from local identification and developing new work.

3. "Let's do *Nutcracker*. We'll get the audience hooked with that, and then they'll want to see *Carmina*." Do audiences cross over? Is *Nutcracker* an event whose purpose is to generate a large part of our earned income? If *Nutcracker* does not sell as well as we hoped, does it mean the organization is not successful in the major focus of its work?

4. "All dance schools make money." A school whose purpose is professional training to feed the company will not only not make money, but will need enormous underwriting. If there is an avocational wing to the school, is the purpose to serve the community or is it to serve as a profit center?

5. "If there are co-artistic directors, shouldn't they direct all of the plays, or, at least, shouldn't each be paid half of what one would cost?" "If we are a repertory dance company, why do we need an artistic director who only choreographs one new work

a season?" An organization's artistic leadership will determine its structure and creative process. The board and community must be educated about the art form and each particular organization's artistic process and goals.

6. Each year, an organization defines its success statistically and against other organizations: "We now have the sixth largest budget in the country, the second largest subscription in the country, and our budget has increased by 18%." However, were goals of the artistic leadership met? Were these increases the result of the work that was created?

MEASURING SUCCESS

The understanding and agreement on evaluation and criteria for measurement of success are essential both to begin the planning process and to assess the plan's success in yearly reviews. Did the organization meet its goals; was it successful in the year just completed? How will the success or lack of success affect the next four years? Should the criteria for measurement be altered?

GETTING THERE: THE RETREAT PROCESS

The best way to achieve understanding and agreement on the evolution, present status, vision, and direction of the organization and on criteria for evaluation is through the retreat process. Here is one possible format for such a retreat.

(Editor's note: Refer also to "Tools for the Planning Process," on page 82.)

FIRST SESSION: Presentation, discussion, understanding and agreement on the evolution, present position, vision and direction, and criteria for measurement of success. This session should not be rushed. As much time as necessary must be taken to ensure that everyone understands and has "bought into" the vision and direction. This understanding serves as the information base for all decisions in the development of the plan.

SECOND SESSION: Usually there are some major non-artistic issues that each organization faces. The full group should discuss these issues at this stage in the planning process. Some examples are: the role of the board; board/staff relations; handling a deficit; fund raising; facility needs; the school; etc. Brainstorming on organization-wide issues and problems will help focus the specific planning committees.

THIRD SESSION: The president of the board charges each of the operational/planning committees (discussed in detail in "Planning by Function" on next page) with its assignment and establishes general time-lines. The committees then meet separately to develop their own timetables and identify key issues. If time permits, the committees can begin their work at this time.

At the conclusion of the retreat, each committee chair reports to the group as a whole on his/her meeting and identifies any issues or questions which have arisen having organizational or intra-committee impact.

WRITING THE PLAN

Now that the organization has reached understanding and agreement on the evolution, the present status, the vision, the direction, and on the criteria to be utilized for evaluation, the organization can begin to write the plan.

A lot of organizations reach this point and believe they already have a plan. Not true — all they have is a statement of objectives. *The plan is the detailed road map, time table, and projection of human and financial resources necessary in order to achieve the vision and goals.* To quote Lewis Carroll in "Alice In Wonderland," "If you don't know where you are going, any road will take you there." Now that we know where we are going, the three partners can begin to make the appropriate map.

THE POSITIONING STATEMENT

The first step is to develop a positioning statement which would include:

1. The mission, a philosophical statement describing the esthetic center of the work.

2. The programs that the organization offers to achieve this vision (productions, outreach, school, touring, classes, etc.)

3. Broad organizational goals.

4. The position of the organization within the community and the art form.

The next step is to develop a very specific plan in each of the functional areas of the organization. These functions will vary from group to group. The range of organizational functions to be considered are the following nine:

A. Artistic

B. Administrative

C. Board

D. Contributed Income

E. Earned income

F. Volunteer Support

G. Facilities

H. School/Training

I. Finance

The staff, board committees, or board special task forces (if no committees exist) are all assigned one or more of the identified functions. Each working group has the agreed-upon information base: the base year, the next year's plan and budget, and the artistic vision and direction at the end of five years.

In essence, the organization is saying: "This is where we are now. This is where we will be in five years. What do we need to do in order to reach that point? What is the order of priority in which things will need to happen? When, in each of the five years, will things need to happen? What are the human and financial needs in order to achieve our vision?"

Each working group is charged with developing its part of the plan and should have appropriate staff support. There needs to be a great deal of communication and give-and-take among the working groups.

ASSEMBLING THE PIECES

The parts of the plan will then be melded into a whole by the executive committee performing the long-range planning function.

If the executive committee is made up of the officers of the board, committee chairs, the artistic and managing directors, and other appropriate staff, this is the point where all the organizational forces connect. It is this executive committee that will be in a position to make hard choices on priorities, time-lines, and budget considerations and to resolve conflicting or overlapping individual functional plans. This is a critical process for the organization, and should have appropriate staff support.

CHECKLIST OF FUNCTIONAL AREAS

The chart that follows is not intended to be an organizational model for a not-for-profit arts organization. The intention is to provoke each organization to ask itself: "Have we identified all of the jobs that need to be done? Have we assigned the job to the appropriate committee or staff person? Who reports to whom?" The chart is also intended to define functions, rather than representing actual committees or staff slots. The chart can serve as a guideline in both the operational and planning process of the organization.

INVOLVING BOARD COMMITTEES IN THE FUNCTIONAL PLANS

Generally, arts organizations have a number of operational board committees. As appropriate, these committees might now assume the planning function as well. Planning, operation, and evaluation must be seen as an ongoing totality, not as separate and unrelated functions.

It may be desirable to add non-board members to some committees to draw on expertise not represented within the organization. An example might be in the area of facilities. A major renovation to the present facility may be under consideration for inclusion in the plan. If such is the case, adding some outside expertise from architects, engineers, contractors, or commercial real estate brokers could furnish important information as a base in this part of the plan.

Each planning group has as its focus the analysis of the size, scope, and shape of its area of concern within the organization in the fifth year. In order to achieve this status, the group needs to determine what actions must be accomplished, and at what expenditure of human and financial resources.

FUNCTIONAL PLANNING TASK FORCES

The following is a discussion of the personnel and the actions involved in the functional planning areas. Not every organization will have these nine areas, and some could have additional functional areas.

A SUGGESTED MODEL OF AN ORGANIZATIONAL STRUCTURE FOR A NOT-FOR-PROFIT ARTS ORGANIZATION

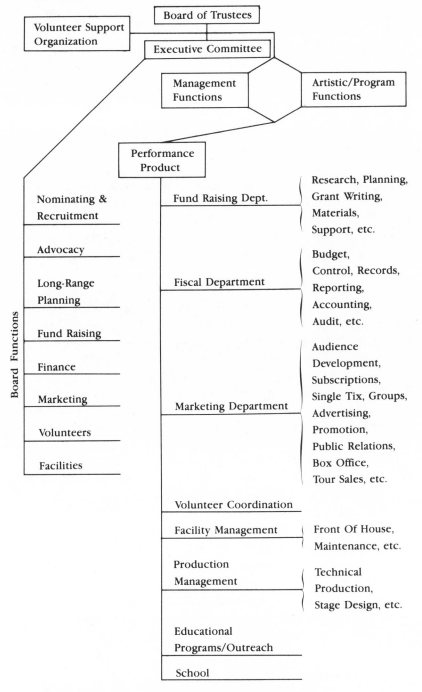

A. ARTISTIC: *Artistic director and artistic staff.* In the development of the two faces of the artistic vision, creative and public, the question was never asked, how? This time, the artistic staff will develop very specific priorities and year-by-year time-lines for actions to achieve the vision. Questions of company, size of company, quality, guest artists, length of rehearsals, number of new works, what will be kept in the repertory, length of season, number of productions, production values, touring, school/training, outreach, and facility must be addressed very specifically. The work of this planning group must be completed and circulated before the other planning groups can begin in-depth work. It is a good idea to present this part of the detailed plan to the board and other staff so that everyone adds this vital dimension to the common information base.

B. ADMINISTRATIVE: *Managing director and the balance of the administrative staff, as appropriate.* Size of staff, level of expertise, present staff potential, future staff growth, appropriate structure, amount of support for department heads, support and direction for the artistic, board, and volunteer areas, and office space, are just some of the concerns that must be addressed.

C. BOARD: *Nominating committee, artistic director, and managing director.* Board expansion, board structure, board expertise, recruiting and motivating board members, board leadership, and board relationship to the professional staff are typical topics for this group.

D. CONTRIBUTED INCOME: *Fund-raising committee, managing director, and development staff.* This group should *not* begin its discussions with: "how much can we raise?" Rather, decisions should be resolved on such items as: what the needs will be, expansion in all areas of the annual giving campaign, board strength and development, debt retirement, capital campaign, building a cash reserve or an endowment, and, ultimately, how all these areas can be addressed through contributed income.

E. EARNED INCOME: *Marketing committee, managing director, and marketing staff.* This group will need to focus on image building, as well as on all aspects of a fully-realized annual marketing campaign. The initial question must not be how many tickets can be sold. Start with the need and make a plan of how to reach that need.

F. VOLUNTEER SUPPORT: *Volunteer leadership, board leadership, and staff liaison*. A not-for-profit arts organization cannot meet its goals without strong, active, and broad-based volunteer support. In a sense, this is a fourth working partner in the organization along with artistic, board, and management leadership. An analysis of the existing volunteer force and the expanded need in year five is required. Questions of structure, size, mission, relationship to board and staff, recruiting, and motivation must be addressed.

G. FACILITIES: *Facility committee and the artistic and managing directors*. Topics for this group include type of space, second stage, studios, shops, new or renovated space, repairs and maintenance, and the like. Facility discussions may extend out past the fifth year. The plan by this planning group may be confined only to maintenance of existing space, while the research and development phase for a new facility might be projected to be completed in years beyond five.

H. SCHOOL: *School committee and the artistic, managing, and school director.* Relationship of school to company, professional training to feed the company, avocational wing, expansion, curriculum, teachers, studio space, locations, self-supporting, profit center, and scholarships, are some of the needs to be discussed and planned by this group.

I. FINANCE: *Finance committee and managing director.* The finance committee is charged with developing the five-year operational income, expense, and capital budget. If there is a deficit, they will also develop a plan for long-term financing, debt service and paydown. They will also discuss any plans for a cash reserve or an endowment.

Remember, no part of planning, operations, and evaluation functions independently. The finance area is the best example of this interdependence. The development of the five-year financial plan, which will serve as the basis for the other functional areas, will require the constant communication to (and among) all the other planning areas. While discussing sections D and E, which deal with Contributed and Earned Income, the suggestion was made not to start with the propositions of how much can be raised or sold. It is in the Finance planning group that these propositions, as well as the plans of these other two groups, must be debated and resolved. The tension between the income portion of the budget on the one hand, and the expense needs of the organization on the other, will be severe. A positive balance must be found between these needs in comparison to reasonable and rational income projections. To over-project income unrealistically can result in deficits; to under-project income deliberately is an abdication of true leadership. When an organization cuts an expense budget, there are usually only three places to cut: the product itself, services to the community, and the marketing of the product. When we reduce any of these, we hinder our ability to generate contributed and earned income. Income projections must be realistic and, at the same time, stretch the organization's commitment from "how little do they, the staff, need to get by?", to "what do we need to grow and develop as an organization?".

THE APPROVED PLAN: A UNITED EFFORT

It is obvious that as the working committees and staff develop their sections of the plan, a great deal of interaction, communication, and give and take must occur. Through this process, everyone in the organization will have contributed to the plan and have a sense of involvement and understanding of the growth and direction of the organization.

As soon as each group has finished its part of the plan, the executive committee, artistic director, and managing director will begin the process of melding them into a whole. Their job is to make final decisions on priorities and timing. When this process is complete, the total plan will be drafted into a whole. This draft will be circulated in advance and then discussed at an extended board meeting. The draft will then be finalized and approved as the five-year plan for growth and development of the organization.

A TIME LINE FOR PLANNING

The entire planning cycle from the initial retreat until final form and development into a prospectus needs to be in a specific and consise time frame. Do not let the process drag out. At the retreat, in addition to charging the committees, the specific schedule should be laid out, and should include:

A. The retreat

B. Initial committee meetings

C. Presentation of the artistic plan

D. Each committee completes its plan

E. The executive committee coordinates and melds it into a draft

F. Presentation and adoption of the draft by the board

G. Final plan written

H. Development of the prospectus and annual report

If at all possible, the process should take no more than four to six months. Anything longer than that, and the work will drift and become unfocused. As well, the common information base may change so that the organization will not be working from the beginning reference point. Most important, the organization needs the plan in order to operate more effectively. The following chart (pages 52–53) is a sketch of the ideal timing and the progression of the planning process.

IMPLEMENTATION: STILL A GROUP ACTIVITY

The first year of the long-term plan is the day-to-day operational plan for the current year. The three organizational partners are responsible for implementing their parts of the plan. This responsibility will also be held jointly by two and three of the partners as their functions interact or overlap (see chart on page 32).

The implementation of the artistic plan must be regarded as a unified activity. The artists should not isolate themselves, even though the nature of creating the work is much more focused internally in the artistic area. A greater interaction is certain to occur between the board and the management leadership.

The day-to-day work of the board is done in comittees. The board

TIME LINE FOR PLANNING

		Approx. 140 days		
	←—15 days—→	←1–3 days→	←30 days→	←45 days—→
AGREEMENT	*PREPARATION*	*RETREAT*	*DEVELOP ARTISTIC PLAN*	*ARTISTIC PLAN ADOPTED*
To Develop Long-Range Plan	Of the Pre-sentation of the Artistic Vi-sion by the Ar-tistic Director	•Evolution •Snapshot of Present Status •Presentation of the Vision •Understanding and Agree-ment •Criteria for Measuring Success ------------------------ •Brainstorm on Key Or-ganizational Issues ------------------------ •Committees Organized ------------------------ •Committees Charged •Identify Key Issues To Address	Begin Work On Functional Area Plans	

	←30 days→		←15 days→	
FUNCTIONAL PLANS COMPLETED	*MELDED INTO A WHOLE*	*ENTIRE BOARD REVIEW & ADOPT*	*FINAL WRITTEN FORM*	*DEVELOP PROSPECTUS*
	by the Executive Committee & Staff			

cannot hope to accomplish its work meeting only as a committee of the whole. The committees are responsible for researching, developing options, structuring campaigns, reporting, and other day-to-day work in their areas. As work is developed, it is shared with other committees when interaction is necessary. When this work requires approval or is a report, it then goes to the executive committee and the board for adoption.

With a small board, these committees may be made up of as few as one or two members. It may be particularly useful to add non-board members to flesh out the committees. This practice serves to: (a) increase the number of people participating in the board leadership, without having too large a board; (b) provide good training and testing of potential board members; and (c) secure an individual's expertise, time, and talent for a specific project when he/she would not otherwise be available for full board service.

The board and its committees must be fully supported by staff. In some functions, the activity may be more of a board function with staff in support—for example, contributed income. In others, it may be more of a staff function with the board committee being a resource—for example, marketing.

Ultimately, however, the day-to-day implementation, operation, and management of the plan is the responsibility of the artistic director, board president, and the managing director. It is interesting to note that this is the same team that was responsible for initiating and sustaining the original planning process.

EVALUATION: THE END, AND THE BEGINNING

Once a year, the organization needs to "call time out" to:

a. reaffirm the artistic vision;

b. evaluate and assess the year just completed (Were goals met? If not, why not?);

c. decide if the remaining four years of the plan need updating or altering in light of the past year and changes in the environment; and

d. agree on the parameters of extending the plan for a new fifth year.

The actual updating and extension of the plan will follow the same pattern pursued by the operational committees and staff in the original planning process.

REAFFIRMING THE VISION

The question will inevitably arise as to when the vision statement should be reviewed and reevaluated. The vision is the constant for the organization; but, at the same time, it is in evolution. It is difficult to find the balance between the course that is chartered and the need for flexibility that is an absolutely essential ingredient in the creative and artistic growth of the organization and in the relationship between the work and the audience.

The vision should never be reevaluated as a negative reaction to a perceived failure, but always in relationship to the criteria for measurement of achievement. Likewise, the work must never be evaluated as a negative reaction to one production or a season, but always in terms of a total body of work over an extended period of time.

Everyone involved with an arts organization must understand the creative process and the different time lines between the artistic and management functions.

With the management function, one-year operational plans, two-year short-term and five-year long-range plans are recommended. This long term thinking is absolutely necessary for organizational stability and growth.

Long-range artistic planning, shapes of season, scale of production, and the like are also essential. However, the artistic process, creating the work itself, lasts a very short period of time immediately preceding the presentation of the work. This process can begin only when the creative team (directors, choreographers, designers, writers, composers, etc.) sit down to create the concept and approach to the particular production or piece. The realization of the work happens when the actors/dancers, writers/composers/musicians, and directors/choreographers actually go into the studio for a relatively brief rehearsal period. Then, of course, how that work is finally shaped by the artists and affected by the audience gives us the completed creation.

It is the board's and management's responsibility to understand the process, create the environment in which the process can flourish, and respond to these discoveries. The response cannot be: "Why can't those artists make up their minds?" Instead, it must be: "How can we find a creative way to respond to the need?"

Once again, a very fine line must be walked between the artistic needs, and the organization's resources and ability to respond to those needs. A positive partnership of the artistic, board, and management leadership will find a way to negotiate this Journey.

PLANNING WHILE MANAGING: "WHAT IF SOMETHING GOES WRONG?"

A question about long-range planning that often arises is, "But what if something goes wrong?" If something does go wrong, don't panic and throw out the plan. Simply go back to the plan and use it as a platform for decision-making. Take the new information and adjust the plan accordingly. If some major change takes place, the organization can more effectively react and continue to control its operation if there is a plan. In the absence of a plan, the organization can only be reactive.

Arts organizations are going to be challenged constantly by unanticipated events — the loss of a major funding source; the subscription campaign does not meet its goal; the facility burns down; the costumes burn up; the chair of the capital campaign is unexpectedly transferred by his/her employer; an unprojected operational deficit occurs; or the artistic director resigns in the middle of the season. *Without* a plan, any of these could be disastrous; *with* a plan, they can be accommodated.

An underlying necessity in all operations is a sound process for making decisions. This process must be clear, precise, formalized, and understood by everyone. It is the absence of a decision-making process which causes confusion and drift within an organization.

To develop a decision-making process, one must consider the following questions:

1. What are the decisions we need to make?

2. What background information do we need in order to make decisions?

3. In what order do decisions need to be made?

4. What are the ramifications of each decision?

5. What other decisions will have to be made as a result?

6. Who is responsible for making decisions?

7. Is approval of the process or of decisions required? If so, by whom?

8. What is the time table for making decisions?

9. Who will implement decisions?

10. Who will communicate decisions and to whom?

CASE IN POINT: THE ARTISTIC DIRECTOR RESIGNS

To illustrate how the presence of a plan and a sound decision-making process allows organizations to deal with unanticipated adversities, take the example of the artistic director resigning in the middle of the season.

The process for coping with this resignation is to develop a short-range plan that includes the following two, primary initiatives:

1. Communicate internally and externally in a very positive way that the change is occuring; explain why.

2. Develop an interim short-term artistic operational plan. Who will function as the day-to-day artistic leader? Will guest directors (choreographers, conductors, etc.) be used for the balance of the season? If the search for a new artistic director will extend into the planning process for the next season, who will make the artistic decisions? If the search should extend into the next season, who will function as the day-to-day artistic leader?

These two initiatives reaffirm that the organization's plan is still clearly in place and allows the rigorous process for identification of a new artistic director to occur.

Unfortunately, most organizations inappropriately appoint a search committee, write a job description, and advertise for a new artistic director. In reality, almost all job descriptions are the same. The organization wants an artistic director who can: direct hit productions with broad audience appeal; work well with people; be an effective community leader; function as a good fund raiser; be realistic and understanding about financial resources; and establish a warm, caring relationship with the board and management. There is no one who can fit this description.

The first step actually should be to develop the profile and define the personality of the job. This process should begin with the remaining two partners, board and management leadership, agreeing on the organizational framework and direction. Does the leadership want to reaffirm the vision for the organization? Does it want to alter the vision in any way? If so, in what way? These decisions must be defined, articulated, understood, and agreed upon before the search process can begin. The range of these choices will be affected by (a) what reasons lay behind the change in leadership; (b) was the person the founding artistic director; and (c) was the director one of a series of leaders in the continuity of the organization?

Consider the example of an organization whose founder is leaving. The question of whether the organization itself should continue needs to be considered. Does the definition of the organization include survival beyond the founding artistic leader's tenure? The organization's only purpose may be to support the vision and the work of the founding artist. If so, then the organization might well go out of existence when he/she decides to stop creating that work.

If the decision is that the organization shall continue, then one of two directions must be taken: (a) the leadership decides on the framework and looks for an artist to fill it; or (b) the leadership looks for an artist who determines the framework that he/she wants as the vision for the organization.

In the first case, the leadership must be unified and very clear in this definition of the vision and framework. The leadership must also know that this is a starting point and that, with a new partner as artistic leader, the vision must and will eventually be evolutionary. In the second case, the board and leadership must be flexible, patient, and be very supportive while this vision is defined, articulated, and realized.

AVOIDING STRESS WHILE GETTING THE JOB DONE

The negative and stressful experiences that organizations and artistic directors have had are due to the lack of definition, understanding, and agreement on a vision and direction. Too often, through a lack of definition or thinking that a different vision might be a good idea, the leadership asks a new artist to define a vision for him/herself, the organization, and the community. It is at this point when the long-range plan must be carefully analyzed and adjusted. The criteria for measurement of success and expectations must be redefined and communicated internally and externally.

In other words, this most basic organizational question of vision and direction must be resolved before the profile and job description can be written and advertised. A part of this discussion must also include the place in the structure for the position. Do the artistic and managing directors have a shared, co-equal responsibility to the board, or is the position to be a producing director with authority and responsibility for both the artistic and managerial functions? Or does the manager have authority and responsibility for both the artistic and managerial functions?

Once agreement is reached on the organizational framework, direction, job description and profile, and the structure, the search can begin for the new third partner. During the interview process, the plan and the above decisions will serve as a base of information for the candidates, as well as containing answers for the hard questions that good candidates will ask.

Once the new artistic director is hired, the planning and operation process continues on the usual ongoing basis.

THE THREE THEMES PLANNING MODEL

Another way to view planning is to see that an organization has three themes running through it.

The first theme is expectations. This theme represents everything the organization is and wants to be. This includes increasing artists' salaries, longer rehearsal periods, capital improvements, reducing a deficit, expanding the subscription base, starting a cash reserve, etc. — everything that is agreed upon as the organization's goals.

The second theme is human resources. This theme represents the artistic board, management, and volunteer support necessary to achieve the expectations/goals of the organization. Also, as a part of this theme, does the organization have the will and commitment to do what is necessary to achieve its goals?

The third theme is the financial resources necessary to achieve the organization's expectations. These include all earned and contributed resources from all sources.

The planning process begins with understanding and agreement being reached on the expectations/goals of the organization. The purpose of planning is to merge the human and financial themes with the expectations/goals theme. Who will do what; what are the necessary financial requirements and resources; and can they meet expectations on a yearly basis?

If at any point the three themes cannot merge, it is not necessary to cut expectations, but to extend expectations over a longer time period.

IN CONCLUSION: PLANNING FOR SUCCESS

In summary, operation, evaluation, and planning are ongoing organization-wide functions. A defined, articulated, understood, agreed-upon vision, direction, and framework are the essential elements for effective planning and sound decision-making. Equally important are agreed-upon and communicated criteria for measurement of success.

A long-range plan is essential for controlled growth and development and for directing and galvanizing everyone's actions toward shared goals. A well thought out plan is liberating for the organization.

Barbara Hauptman

PLANNING — A MANAGER'S PERSONAL POINT OF VIEW

L ike many of you, I am not an accountant. I have never even taken an accounting course. I learned about finance and budgets out of one basic emotion—fear. Like Scarlett O'Hara and the radishes, I have always sworn, "I'll never go hungry again." I used to do amazing financial figuring on subways. I would work out my expenses and then subtract my income. By the Fourteenth Street stop, I would be absolutely terrified. This was my first lesson in DEFICIT SPENDING.

BARBARA HAUPTMAN is currently Vice President, Manager of Daytime Programming with Saatchi & Saatchi Compton Advertising. Prior to S. & S. Compton, she was the director of Operations of the Theatre Development Fund for three years. Ms. Hauptman joined the Twyla Tharp Dance Company as Executive Director in 1979. She produced Twyla Tharp on Broadway in 1980 and assisted in *Confessions of a Corner Maker*, CBS/Cable. From 1976 to 1979 she was an arts analyst in the Theatre Program for the New York State Council on the Arts. She was Managing Director for the Urban Arts Corps Theatre and the Bil Baird Marionettes as well as co-founder of Management Services for the Performing Arts. At the Williamstown Theatre Festival, she was General Manager for two summer seasons.

When it came to the financial aspect of the theatre and dance companies for which I worked, I functioned somewhat similarly. I religiously wrote down all the expenses and then subtracted the income. Once again fear set in. So I began to learn about fundraising, donative intent, and judicious expense cutting.

As I began to fundraise, I realized that most funders were interested in funding projects rather than general operating, so I began to budget activities separately as well as parts of the whole operation, only to discover that what I had learned to do was called FUND ACCOUNTING.

Thus, I learned about finance as the circumstances required. However, in the process, I began to realize that being at ease with money made me feel confident and made it easier to communicate with my Board, Funding Sources, and Artistic Director. I lost my fear of money. After all, $10.00 can be a cool million by adding a mere five zeroes.

I came to planning for many of the same reasons. I realized that by thinking ahead and not continually living from day to day, it became easier to communicate my needs, especially the financial ones. Planning, I discovered, was really just thinking and staying alert.

In the performing arts business, we often fall into the trap of believing we are magicians. The stage is so often filled with magic, that we, as managers, begin to believe that we can transform a company into a business by our own effort alone. This kind of thinking tends to make one most overwrought, because magic is unfortunately not a good substitute for planning. Planning sounds like a bugaboo. Planning is for corporations, not for artists, we say.

Planning does, however, help ease the masochistic sensibility we often have. It is one thing to have an accounting system that is not-for-profit; it is another to have a not-for-profit mentality.

With clearly thought-out planning, one does not have to wait for the grant that may not come. One can be prepared and flexible enough to continue to further the mission of the organization. With planning, the anxiety of "how can we," "will we," and "who will pay" is eliminated, and the creative process allowed to flourish.

The plan becomes the visual rendering of the goals of the organization for the short and long term. *The presentation on paper* is critical. Your thoughts are easier to communicate when written down. Your Board and Funding Sources, most of whom are associated with the for-profit world, will be more comfortable with a well written, carefully organized plan. Use declarative sentences. Charts can be helpful.

In corporate enterprise, strategy statements, company objectives, and project goals are always formally presented — even if only three lines on a piece of paper. Once this document is circulated and read, the dialogue between the organization and its Board can begin. The foundation from which agreement can be reached about the long range plans for the future is established.

In the planning process the last step should be the numbers. Money should not be the issue in the initial planning stages, since the mention of money can be inhibiting. CATEGORIES are the first critical element in budgeting for both the short and long term. The categories of your budget represent the intentions of the organization. The lengthy narrative of the plan converts to simple categories. For example, if an organization's mission is to be involved in the development of new writers for the theatre, the budget categories should reflect this endeavor with categories for writer payments and expenses. Without these categories, the organization looks like a traditional theatre and not a home to new voices in the theatre. The amount of money allocated to these categories is not the issue at present. The intention to be seriously committed to new writers is emphasized and reinforced by including the categories in the budget. The expenditures for writers can be developed as the organization grows and since it is clearly a priority, the amount of these payments will naturally increase over the years of the plan.

If you plan to pay artists or others presently working for little or no payment, put it in your budget. At this juncture, we are not concerned about whether the organization can afford to pay them or how much; we are presenting the *intention to do so*. Your categories will probably increase as they are applied to all the years of your plan. This visual application year by year in chart form begins to show the growth of the organization. All before any numbers are supplied.

Exhibit A (page 68) is a budget form devised by Sander Gossard & Associates, Inc. for FEDAPT which could be a useful guide in establishing the categories for your company. Include your artistic director and staff in the formulation of categories. Leaving out an item can be more crippling than having too little money overall. Remember your mission, so carefully constructed in narrative form, must translate into budgetary categories.

After establishing categories for the income and expense portion of your budget, ASSUMPTIONS must be formulated as you supply the numbers. For example, BOX OFFICE REVENUE: Will one assume 75%

of paid gross capacity or 60% or 50% and why was a particular percentage chosen? History of the organization may be cited or strength of box office appeal for a certain play, actor, ballet, etc. Whatever reason is used, it becomes the assumption or rationale for the dollar figure in the budget. A good financial plan will have an assumption behind every number on its budget sheets. The budgets should be accompanied by written assumptions whenever possible; these will facilitate your communication with your Board or Finance Committee. Exhibit B (page 80) is an example of an assumption statement.

In both short and long range financial planning, ALTERNATIVES must enter the picture and be carefully considered by the staff and Board of the organization. I have found that most Board members, Funders, and Advisors do not really want to say "no" to a plan or proposal. Often they refrain from saying anything, leaving the organization totally in the dark as to what step to take next. Therefore, in your planning/budgeting process, line up your options and alternatives so that the Board will be given the opportunity to see the various "what ifs" and thereby help you make planning decisions. Analyzing options is easier and more productive than having to say "no, we do not have the money to do this." The planning process then becomes about choosing one option over another.

A plan should contain many "what ifs" or MULTI-SCENARIOS. The best example I can give is culled from my experience producing Twyla Tharp Dance on Broadway in 1980. The company had never self-produced and a three-week debut season on Broadway was a major undertaking. Our annual operating budget had to be increased nearly 100% to accomplish all that Twyla Tharp wanted to achieve for this three-week engagement. The biggest expense was a major full evening piece Twyla was creating. I began to actively fund raise and we set the plan into motion. As the time drew near to making space, labor, and production commitments, I knew we were not going to be able to present the season as originally planned. I dreaded telling Twyla "no." So once again in a panic, I discovered the "multi-scenario" approach to making planning decisions. I simply put together four budgets: DREAM, COMPROMISE, REPERTORY, and NO SEASON. Each budget represented the entire fiscal year with the Broadway "project" reflected in four different ways. Since the Twyla Tharp Dance Foundation is an on-going organization with year round commitments, the Broadway adventure could only be viewed as a part of the whole, and its income and expenses amortized across the entire fiscal year.

I listed the expenses as follows:

A. DREAM: as if we had all the money in the world and could do the season as we had "dreamed";

B. COMPROMISE: a realistic look at the cost of the new full evening work, modifying many of the production elements;

C. REPERTORY: completely eliminating the new piece and presenting only works from the existing Tharp repertory for the three-week Broadway engagement;

D. NO SEASON: completely eliminating the New York City Season on Broadway and concentrating on touring and rehearsing the company.

I then applied the income to each scenario. I had projections or actual figures on what I could raise and felt somewhat comfortable with projecting box office revenue at 50% of paid gross capacity. Remember, many of my real and anticipated grants were geared specifically to the Broadway season.

What I discovered I still marvel at today. My worst budget was NO SEASON. Since much of my income projection was based on the revenue, both earned and in contributions earmarked to support the Broadway season, eliminating it altogether made the fiscal picture for the year much bleaker. I was greatly relieved. I then knew that what we had started had to be finished. I also had a visual tool with which to convince my Board that the money had to be found to continue. Exhibit C (page 81) is a graphic display of how these alernatives can be presented.

The next worst budget was the DREAM. No surprise there. I had included in that budget those luxury items I knew we would be economically foolish to entertain. My most reasonable and clearly obtainable budget was REPERTORY. It was almost a breakeven, but clearly not an artistic challenge for either Twyla personally, or for the company. With this chart in hand I called a meeting with Twyla and Santo Loquasto, our set and costume designer. Although not a pleasant meeting to hold, I felt I had done my homework. I presented my chart (my set of alternatives) and explained the assumptions I had used to obtain the categories and numbers. The discussion was then opened and we all pondered our options. Clearly sound business sense directed us toward REPERTORY, but Twyla felt that *artistically* the company could not premiere on Broadway without a major new work. We all agreed. We, therefore, committed ourselves to the COMPROMISE alternative. Twyla and Santo agreed to re-think the new piece in terms of sets and costumes, and I agreed to get the Board's commitment to raise the necessary dollars. We all agreed to stretch to make the COMPROMISE work. The moral to this story is that planning coupled with alternative suggestions can facilitate decision making without ever having to use the word, "no."

I was able to take this same scenario to the Board and solicit their co-operation. I could easily explain the assumptions used, the alternatives from a *financial and artistic* point of view, and the risk being undertaken. We did succeed with our COMPROMISE plan.

Opening night on Broadway at the Winter Garden Theatre, Santo Loquasto said, "I want to thank you." I said, "Why?", and he replied, "The day I realized that there had to be a compromise is when I had a good idea on how to do this piece." I was truly touched. By putting an effort into outlining a plan, I had actually effected the creative process. That pleased me. It also pleased me that the Twyla Tharp Dance Company completed an artistically and financially successful run on Broadway and ended the fiscal year in a NET CURRENT ASSET POSITION.

The multi-scenario approach can be applied to five year planning as well. One can construct the scenarios in many different ways. First the proper assumptions have to be agreed upon and then the scenarios outlined and finally the numbers added. One may plan a series of projects and then construct varying scenarios on which years the activities will take place. The calendar will begin to dictate many alternatives. If one lists all the activities that the organization would like to accomplish in the next five years, the calendar could pose more problems than dollars and cents.

As one begins to make decisions about when to do certain projects, the assumptions for the various scenarios are beginning to take place. Dance companies, for example, will always want to do a major season, tour internationally and domestically, and perhaps have a long term residency on a college campus. A calendar will quickly indicate the difficulty in accomplishing such an agenda in one fiscal year. The company can then prioritize its goals and phase the activities over a number of years.

Remember financial planning is a valuable tool for *interpreting* your organization's mission in terms of numbers rather than words. It is nothing to fear or dread. Once you begin to think in terms of categories, assumptions, alternatives, and multi-scenarios, you will be a planner armed with the ability to help yourself as well as generate constructive help from others.

Planning will put your organization on the road to financial stability. It will help you gain confidence as a manager and make dialogues among you and your Board, funders, and audiences far easier. You do not have to be a financial wizard to plan. A good calculator and an open mind is all that is required. My best wishes to all of you.

EXHIBIT A

These budget forms are guides, not blueprints, and were prepared as a reference for any kind of operation. They contain certain line items not applicable to all operations and may not have included certain line items for other operations.

Prepared by Sander Gossard & Associates, Inc., Bronx, N.Y.

I. PHYSICAL PRODUCTION

		Prep	Put-In	Running	Take-Out	Total
	SCENERY					
	SOFT GOODS & DRAPERIES					
	MECHANICALS					
	PROPS					
	PERISHABLE PROPS					
E X P E N S E S	LIGHTING EQUIPMENT					
	LAMPS					
	SOUND EQUIPMENT					
	FILM & PROJECTION EQUIPMENT					
	COSTUMES					
	SHOES					
	WIGS					
	MAKEUP					
	MISCELLANEOUS					
	SUBTOTAL					

I. PHYSICAL PRODUCTION

		Prep	Put-In	Running	Take-Out	Total
S E R V I C E S	TRUCKING					
	WASTE REMOVAL					
	MISCELLANEOUS					
	SUBTOTAL					
C R E A T I V E F E E S / S A L A R I E S	SET DESIGNER					
	ASSISTANT SET DESIGNER(S)					
	DRAFTSMEN					
	LIGHTING DESIGNER					
	ASSISTANT LIGHTING DESIGNER(S)					
	COSTUME DESIGNER					
	ASSISTANT COSTUME DESIGNER(S)					
	GRAPHICS DESIGNER					
	FILM/PROJECTION DESIGNER					
	HAIRSTYLIST					
	MAKEUP DESIGNER					
	MISCELLANEOUS					
	SUBTOTAL					

Physical production continued on next page.

I. PHYSICAL PRODUCTION cont'd

		Prep	*Put-In*	*Running*	*Take-Out*	*Total*
TECHNICAL FEES/SALARIES	TECHNICAL DIRECTOR					
	CARPENTER					
	ASSISTANT CARPENTER(S)					
	ELECTRICIAN					
	ASSISTANT ELECTRICIAN(S)					
	PROPERTY MAN					
	ASSISTANT PROPERTY MEN					
	SOUND MAN					
	FLY MEN					
	STAGEHANDS					
	TECHNICAL ADVISOR(S)					
	WARDROBE SUPERVISOR					
	WARDROBE ASSISTANTS					
	HAIRDRESSERS					
	MAKEUP ARTISTS					
	MISCELLANEOUS					
	SUBTOTAL					
	TOTAL PHYSICAL PRODUCTION					

II. PERFORMANCE

	Prep	Put-In	Running	Take-Out	Total
EXPENSES					
PLAY ROYALTIES					
AUDITION/CASTING EXPENSES					
SCRIPTS					
REHEARSAL SPACE					
MISC. REHEARSAL EXPENSES					
MISCELLANEOUS					
SUBTOTAL					
FEES/SALARIES					
CASTING DIRECTOR					
DIRECTOR					
ASSISTANT DIRECTOR(S)					
CHOREOGRAPHER					
DANCE CAPTAIN					
STAGE MANAGER					
ASSISTANT STAGE MANAGER(S)					
CAST					
CHORUS					
UNDERSTUDIES/ STANDBYS					
MISCELLANEOUS					
SUBTOTAL					

Performance continued on next page.

II. PERFORMANCE cont'd

	Prep	Put-In	Running	Take-Out	Total
MUSIC ROYALTIES					
COPYING					
INSTRUMENT RENTAL					
REHEARSAL SPACE					
MISC. REHEARSAL EXPENSES					
MISCELLANEOUS					
SUBTOTAL					
MUSIC ARRANGER					
VOCAL ARRANGER/COACH					
REHEARSAL PIANIST					
CONDUCTOR					
MUSICIANS					
MISCELLANEOUS					
SUBTOTAL					
TOTAL PERFORMANCE					

(MUSIC EXPENSES — rows from MUSIC ROYALTIES through first SUBTOTAL)

(MUSICAL FEE/SAL. — rows from MUSIC ARRANGER through second SUBTOTAL)

III. ADMINISTRATIVE

	Prep	Put-In	Running	Take-Out	Total
OFFICE RENTAL					
OFFICE SUPPLIES					
UTILITIES					
TELEPHONE					
POSTAGE					
MESSENGER SERVICE					
TRANSPORTATION					
SUBSCRIPTION					
MONEY-RAISING EXPENSES					
INSURANCES (EQUITY, FLOATER, WORKERS' COMPENSATION, LIABILITY, ETC.)					
ENTERTAINMENT					
MISCELLANEOUS					
SUBTOTAL					

(Left margin vertical label: EXPENSES)

Adminstrative continued on next page.

III. ADMINISTRATIVE cont'd

		Prep	Put-In	Running	Take-Out	Total
FEES/SALARIES	MANAGING DIRECTOR					
	ARTISTIC DIRECTOR					
	GENERAL MANAGER					
	MEMBERSHIP DIRECTOR					
	SUBSCRIPTION DIRECTOR					
	FUND RAISING/ DEVELOPMENT DIR.					
	PRODUCTION SECRETARY					
	PRODUCTION ASSISTANTS					
	SECRETARIAL					
	BOOKKEEPER(S)					
	LEGAL FEES					
	ACCOUNTANTS					
	MISCELLANEOUS					
	SUBTOTAL					
TAXES & FUNDS	PAYROLL TAX					
	STATE TAX					
	CITY TAX					
	OCCUPANCY TAX					
	PENSION					
	WELFARE					
	VACATION					
	PER DIEMS					
	MISCELLANEOUS					
	SUBTOTAL					
	TOTAL ADMINISTRATIVE					

IV. ADVERTISING & PROMOTION

	Prep	Put-In	Running	Take-Out	Total
EXPENSES					
NEWSPAPERS					
TELEVISION					
RADIO					
POSTERS					
PHOTOGRAPHS					
SIGNS					
PRINTING					
FLYERS					
MAILINGS					
HOUSE BOARDS					
MISCELLANEOUS					
SUBTOTAL					
FEES/SALARY					
PUBLIC RELATIONS DIRECTOR					
PRESS & PROMOTIONS DIRECTOR					
POSTER/LOGO DESIGNER					
MISCELLANEOUS					
SUBTOTAL					
TOTAL ADVERTISING & PROMOTION					

V. THEATRE/HOUSE

		Prep	Put-In	Running	Take-Out	Total
EXPENSES	THEATRE ADVANCES					
	THEATRE RENTAL					
	MARQUIS					
	DISPLAY					
	TICKETS					
	PROGRAMS					
	BOX OFFICE EXPENSES					
	UTILITIES					
	TELEPHONE					
	MAINTENANCE EQUIPMENT					
	MAINTENANCE PERISHABLES					
	MISCELLANEOUS					
	SUBTOTAL					
FEES/SALARIES	HOUSE MANAGER					
	BOX OFFICE MANAGER					
	BOX OFFICE ASSISTANTS					
	USHERS					
	SECURITY PERSONNEL					
	JANITORIAL/ MAINTENANCE PERSONNEL					
	MISCELLANEOUS					
	SUBTOTAL					
	TOTAL THEATRE/HOUSE					

VI. RETURNABLE BONDS & DEPOSITS

		Prep	Put-In	Running	Take-Out	Total
MISCELLANEOUS	STAGE HANDS					
	ACTORS' EQUITY					
	MUSICIANS					
	THEATRE					
	TRAVEL/ TRANSPORTATION					
	A.T.P.A.M.					
	TREASURERS					
	MISCELLANEOUS					
	SUBTOTAL					
	CONTINGENCY					
	TOTAL RETURNABLE BONDS/DEP.					

TOTALS

	Prep	Put-In	Running	Take-Out	Total
EXPENSES SUBTOTAL					
SERVICES SUBTOTAL					
CREATIVE FEES/ SALARIES SUBTOTAL					
TECHNICAL FEES/ SALARIES SUBTOTAL					
TOTAL PHYSICAL PRODUCTION					
EXPENSES SUBTOTAL					
FEES/SALARIES SUBTOTAL					
MUSIC EXPENSES SUBTOTAL					
MUSIC FEES/SALARIES SUBTOTAL					
TOTAL PERFORMANCE					
EXPENSES SUBTOTAL					
FEES/SALARIES SUBTOTAL					
TAXES & FUNDS SUBTOTAL					
TOTAL ADMINISTRATIVE					

TOTALS cont'd

	Prep	Put-In	Running	Take-Out	Total
EXPENSES SUBTOTAL					
FEES/SALARIES SUBTOTAL					
TOTAL ADVERTISING & PROMOTION					
EXPENSES SUBTOTAL					
FEES/SALARIES SUBTOTAL					
TOTAL THEATRE/HOUSE					
MISCELLANEOUS SUBTOTAL					
CONTINGENCY					
TOTAL RETURNABLE BONDS/DEP.					
GRAND TOTAL					

EXHIBIT B

ASSUMPTIONS FOR A BUDGET (A SAMPLING)

Attachment Explaining Specific Entries in the Accompanying 1985/86 Budget.

REVENUE
  Earned Income

Box Office Sales	Based on 50% Paid Capacity, for 3 Programs, 4 Weeks Each. 1984/85 season was at 52%.
Touring Fees	Based on 14 Weeks at 80% of Stated Fees 1984/85 season was 16½ Weeks at 75%.

  Contributed Income

State Arts Council	Based on Anticipated $1,500 Increase Over 1984/85. Same increase as last year. Council staff indicates positive audits and supportive panelists.
City Funding	Based on 5% Increase over 1984/85. City has 8% budget surplus to spend, but Mayor is antagonistic; City Council members are supporters/subscribers, we should get something.
XYZ Foundation	Based on conversations with staff officer. $10,000 New Grant. They asked us to apply, and have history of funding programs like our school tours. $10,000 is 35% of program's cost.

EXPENSES
  Personnel

Artists' Salaries	Based on 12 Artists @ $500/wk × 3 Programs × (4 Performance + 3 Rehearsal) Weeks, + 22% PRT & Benefits (FICA, Workers' Comp, Unemployment Insurance, Pension & Welfare, etc.).
Administrative Staff	Based on Present Staff Plus One Assistant, × 6% Cost Of Living Increase.
Advertising	Based on Daily Newspaper Display Ads, every day during run of show.

  Production

Running Expendables	Based on Last Year + 10%.

EXHIBIT C

MULTI-SCENARIO APPROACH TO MAKING PLANNING DECISIONS
Twyla Tharp Dance, Winter Garden Theatre (Broadway) Season, 1980

DREAM	COMPROMISE	REPERTORY	NO SEASON
Income based on 50% box office. Foundation, corporate and government support for a three week season, a major new piece, and repertory.	Income based on 50% box office. Foundation, corporate and government support for a three week season, a new piece and repertory.	Income based on 50% box office. Foundation, corporate and government support for a three week season of TTD repertory.	Income based on eliminating box office revenue and all grants/contributions toward NYC Season. Only touring income and general operating funds remain.
Expenses based on an elaborate set/costumes for major new piece, major "new wave" composer, and well-known writer.	Expenses based on modifying the new piece in terms of the production values, composer and writer fees.	Expenses based on complete elimination of new piece. Repertory expenses incurred in previous fiscal years.	Expenses based on touring, rehearsing, and general operating.
Deficit – Extensive	Deficit – Manageable	Deficit – Almost Breakeven	Deficit – Extensive*

* Eliminating season's potential earned and contributed income seriously hampered ability to amortize general operating expenses over the fiscal year.

Frederic B. Vogel

TOOLS FOR THE PLANNING PROCESS

I n any kind of endeavor there are obstacles, snags and quandaries that seem somehow monumental. While planning *No Quick Fix (Planning)*, two quotations keep running through my mind:

"For want of a horseshoe, a kingdom was lost."

'The best laid plans of mice and men so often go awry."

I feel that, unless an organization embarks on planning which I view as "the horseshoe," there will be a definite "loss of kingdom." As far as I am concerned, that is a simple, either/or situation.

As for the "best laid plans" quandary, the following section should be of help. The retreat process documented is a potent means of getting the good intentions "of mice and men" to reach fruition.

FREDERIC B. VOGEL — During his tenure (since 1970) as Executive Director of the Foundation for the Extension and Development of the American Professional Theatre, FEDAPT has offered Management Technical Assistance in all aspects of administration to over 300 not-for-profit theatre and dance companies, and performing arts centers.

Prior to heading FEDAPT, Mr. Vogel was Assisting Director of the Performing Arts Division at the 1962 Seattle World's Fair which presented more than 125 international theatrical and concert attractions. He was in charge of the

---

In the next section, the Basic Logical Outline (Exhibit D) for evaluating a project/program should serve as a map for clear and cool thinking, during the retreat process; while actually drafting the plan; and during the implementation phase after planning is completed.

The charts of the hypothetical Aardvark Dance Theatre (Exhibits E and F) created by Nello McDaniel are examples of how simple the plan can look, and how fundamental these ideas are to the life of an organization. I believe they serve to convince anyone that planning is an artist's — hence, an arts organization's — best friend.

FEDAPT'S RETREAT PROCESS

A performing arts organization or other not-for-profit organization interested in beginning the planning process may need some assistance in galvanizing the artistic leadership, management leadership, and board leadership into beginning the process. This may be true for both very large and very small organizations. One of the major obstacles may simply be getting all the concerned parties together in one place at the same time so that they may discuss the organization's areas of concern, operational systems, and most importantly, to establish the desired context for evaluating the work of the organization.

A retreat provides the opportunity to do exactly that. It brings all of the concerned parties together, at a neutral place and time, away from telephones, spouses, children, and other assorted distractions, for the single-minded purpose of discussing the organization.

It may seem obvious, but it cannot be over-emphasized that the main concern in holding a retreat is that everyone involved in the organization's decision-making process is brought together at the *same time* to share the *same information*.

It should be clearly articulated to all that planning is designed to refine the decision-making process, and not to decide who should be

---

international Special Events Program, and served as the Director of the Film Program which premiered films from the world over. Mr. Vogel was subsequently appointed Special Events Director by the New York State Commission on the World's Fair for the New York State Pavilion at that World's Fair, a position he held from 1963 through 1965. As General Manager for LUMADRAMA (a "son et lumiere") at Independence Hall in Philadelphia, Mr. Vogel coordinated this tourist and educational program with the U.S. Department of the Interior and was responsible for its operation.

fired, or who should leave the board! The *groundrule* is that there are *no hidden agendas!*

FEDAPT has been conducting retreats since the mid-1970's and, as a result of trial and error, chooses to use an organizational self-analysis approach. Responsible and experienced consultants, other than FEDAPT, can also be called upon to conduct the process.

FEDAPT strongly recommends the use of *two* consultants:

1. The Interviewer, who gathers background information from the participants. The interviewer should be thoroughly experienced in, and knowledgeable of, the artistic discipline involved.

2. The Facilitator, who will actually guide the retreat itself, should be conversant with the nature and dynamics of not-for-profit boards and organizations, as well as being perceptive of general group dynamics.

There are four main parts of the retreat process: research, interviews, the retreat itself, and the written follow-up report or planning outline.

1. THE RESEARCH. The following information should be supplied to the consultants before they begin:

a. A copy of the original Articles of Incorporation, and amendments.

b. The most recent independent audits, at least for the last two years.

c. Any other financial statements and information on the program.

Beginning his theatrical career as an actor at age nine, Mr. Vogel appeared on Broadway, off-Broadway, the summer stock circuit, television and film before switching his creative priorities to the "front office." He has held administrative positions in summer theatres, music tents, off-Broadway theatres and created and supervised Broadway Theatre Leagues (Columbia Artists Management) from North Carolina to Oregon, from Texas to British Columbia. For several years Mr. Vogel served as an Arts Management consultant to and for a variety of theatrical organizations. He was one of the first

d. A list of the board members indicating their backgrounds, professional qualifications, and terms on the board.

e. Information on whatever board committees exist.

f. A staff organizational chart listing job descriptions and areas of responsibility.

If any of this information does not exist, care must be taken to create it before the process begins. If it simply cannot be acquired, the absence of this information should be a topic of discussion at the retreat.

2. THE INTERVIEW. During the two or three days before the retreat itself, the consultants meet with all board and staff members, if possible. Each interview should last about 45 minutes, and not more than one person should be interviewed at a time. The Interviewer conducts this portion of the process, but the Facilitator, who should always be present, may ask questions as well. Each interviewee is asked the same questions:

· What is the purpose of the organization?

· What do you feel is the project's major area of concern? (problem? weakness? etc.)

· Why are you in the board (or on the staff)?

· What would you like the organization to be, or do, or become?

Other questions are added, depending on what preliminary discussions with the manager (or Board chairman) turn up, or what is indicated by studying the written material presented. These interviews are conducted on perhaps Tuesday, Wednesday and Thursday

---

professionals to be invited to offer Technical Assistance Consultancies by the New York State Council on the Arts.

In addition, he has been a Stage Manager, Box Office Treasurer, Subscription and Group Sales Manager, PR/Publicity Director, General Manager and Producer. He has lectured at the leading university arts management graduate programs in the United States including Yale, University of Wisconsin, New York University, Brooklyn College and State University of New York at Binghampton.

(or, if a smaller cast of characters is involved, on Wednesday and Thursday only). Friday morning, the Interviewer and Facilitator should be free to plan the retreat to follow.

3. THE RETREAT ITSELF. The retreat should be conducted from early Friday afternoon continuously until late Saturday afternoon (or Saturday afternoon to late Sunday afternoon). All key staff members and board members should be present. To keep the group manageable, the number of participants should be limited to about 25-30.

4. THE WRITTEN FOLLOW-UP REPORT. A detailed written report should be presented to the organization (copy to the artistic director, manager, and to the board chairman) within three weeks following the retreat. It is this document which serves as the guideline for embarking on the actual process of determining and writing the plan.

Some additional points to consider:

1. A Board Retreat is designed to investigate the basic purposes, the identity, the dynamic — in short, the *mission* of the organization. A total evaluation of the operation should be addressed and, in addition, its objectives, its goals and its concerns.

2. A Retreat is most productive if the core of the Board and top salaried staff attend for the *entire* scheduled time.

3. Retreats are more productive if an over-night stay is included in the plan (i.e., begin on a Friday afternoon about 3:00 pm, going to 10:30 pm or so, with a dinner break; commencing the following morning at 9:00 am, after breakfast, through lunch and ending at 3:00 or 4:00 pm that Saturday afternoon).

4. There should be no outside influences such as spouses, guests, telephone calls, cooking or other household chores. This would mean that a conference center, lodge, motel, etc. serving meals is the best retreat site.

5. The presence of a facilitator is imperative. As stated, for an arts organization this should be someone with an arts sensibility who is in no way connected with the company or with members of the Board. If you accept FEDAPT's suggestion of an Interviewer/Facilitator team, then both should be present.

6. A retreat is not a formal Board meeting. It results in identifying consensus and is not designed for voting by-laws, amendments, etc. Should there be issues identified in the retreat which require Board vote, a formal Board meeting should be scheduled following the retreat to take such action.

7. Ideally, the 25–30 people present at the retreat should be the most involved—the "movers and shakers." At least the Artistic Director, Managing Director, and the Board's Executive Committee should be present. The potential participants at a retreat should be discussed with the consultants to determine the final cast of characters.

8. When the organization receives the written report which is composed of evaluations and recommendations from both consultants, the organization should be ready to embark on the actual "Planning" process.

BASIC LOGICAL OUTLINE FOR EVALUATION

The "Criteria For Evaluating A Future Project/Program" which follows is a useful tool both during the retreat, and the planning and implementation phases which follow. It can be used as a "yardstick" to measure the basic value of ideas and actions, and whether they are appropriate for the organization to pursue.

EXHIBIT D
CRITERIA FOR EVALUATING A FUTURE PROJECT/PROGRAM

CONSISTENCY:

Is it consistent with the organization's mission?

NEED:

Is there a need in the general community?

Is there a need in the arts (theatre, dance, music, etc.) community?

Is there a need within the organization?

DEMAND:

Who will this serve? How many?

Who wants it to happen?

QUALITY:

Does it have the potential to be a project of sufficient quality?

TRACK RECORD OF PERSONNEL INVOLVED:

Can we depend on those with whom we would be working? What is their work load?

Do they have experience with such projects and the necessary skills?

ROLE:

What is the organization's specific role in the project?

EFFECT ON ARTS COMMUNITY:

Is this controversial? Is it worth it in spite of "mixed reviews" or "mixed reactions"?

PRECEDENT:

What kind of precedent will this set for the future in our organization?

What about the general arts community and the community at large?

PRACTICALITY:

Does it fall within our definition of "reasonable cost"?

Is it realistic?

Does the organization have the resources (time, energy, personnel, funding)?

Is the organization willing and able to seek additional resources (funding, personnel, time, energy)?

Is this a good time to schedule this?

SAMPLE PLANNING OUTLINE, AND SAMPLE ACTION PLAN

As the result of the hypothetical Aardvark Dance Theatre retreat, the planning process began. The results are summarized in the Sample Planning Outline (Exhibit F) which follows.

Notice that Aardvark has established a single, three-year objective in each of four categories, based on a one-sentence Mission Statement. It determined a goal for each objective, during each of the three years of the plan, which it will use to measure "success."

"Exhibit E" is a Sample Action Plan. This has taken one goal, for one year of the plan, and sketched out a specific strategy for reaching the goal. A similar Action Plan was developed for each goal during each of the three years. Viewing all of these Action Plans together gives one a fully detailed plan of attack to meet Aardvark Dance Theatre's long-range objectives.

EXHIBIT E

OBJECTIVE: To enrich the lives of the people of the region by providing them with the opportunity to experience the company in performance on tour.

GOAL: Six weeks of touring in 1986–87. Primary Responsibility: Exec. Director.

STRATEGY: Increase the awareness of Aardvark's quality and availability through a marketing plan structured to insure six weeks of touring in 1986–87.

DATE	TASK	PRIMARY RESPONSIBILITY	CONSULT/ ASSIST	REVIEW/ APPROVE/ EVALUATE
6/86	Set fee structure for 86–87 touring season	Exec. Dir.	Dev. Dir.	Finance Committee
7/86	Prepare mailing piece to entice potential Aardvark sponsors	Exec. Dir.	Free lance designer	
8/86	Review available mailing list—determine Aardvark targets	Exec. Dir.	Sect'y.	
9/86	Mail Aardvark brochure to 1,000 potential sponsors	Sect'y.		
9/86	Hire P/T booking asst. for six months	Exec. Dir.		Exec. Committee
9/15-12/86	Call all 1,000 sponsors to determine potential Aardvark interest	Booking Asst.	Exec. Dir.	Review ea. week for 100 contacts
12/1-5	Determine areas of greatest Aardvark interest	Exec. Dir.	Booking Asst.	

DATE	TASK	PRIMARY RESPON- SIBILITY	CONSULT/ ASSIST	REVIEW/ APPROVE/ EVALUATE
12/5-10	Send second mailing to targeted areas (due to over- whelming response—see you at ACUCAA)	Exec. Dir.		
12/18- 22	Attend ACUCAA con- ference and concentrate on block-booking consortia	Exec. Dir./ Booking Asst.		
1/87	Develop poten- tial tour itinery based on spon- sor interest	Exec. Dir.	Booking Asst.	
1/87	Develop budget for proposed consortia tour	Exec. Dir.	Booking Asst.	Finance Committee/Exec. Committee
2/87	Explore poten- tial contributed income for consortia tour	Devel. Dir.	Board	
3/87	Negotiate con- tracts w/Aardvark sponsors	Exec. Dir.		
4-6/87	Pursue addi- tional sponsors via telephone to fill in for open dates (any holes in the tour)	Exec. Dir.	Sect'y.	
6/87	Propose tour as part of official budget for 86-87	Exec. Dir.		Board

EXHIBIT F   AARDVARK DANCE THEATRE — SAMPLE PLANNING OUTLINE

	1985–86 GOALS, YEAR 1	1986–87 GOALS, YEAR 2	1987–88 GOALS, YEAR 3
ARTISTIC			
— Dancers	8 on contract	10 on contract	14 on contract
— New Work	Commission 4 new works	Commission 2 new works Art. Dir. makes 1 new work	Commission 2 new works Art. Dir. makes 1 new work Mount a new Nutcracker
PERFORMANCE	1 home season/4 perfs.	2 home seasons/10 perfs.	2 home seasons/12 perfs. 12 Nutcrackers
TOURING	4 weeks	6 weeks	6 weeks
MANAGEMENT/ PERSONNEL	1 Exec. Dir./1 secty. (p.t.)	Exec. Dir./Dev. Dir. (f.t.) secretary (f.t.)	Exec. Dir./Dev. Dir. secty./Bus. Mgr. (f.t.)
ETC.	etc.	etc.	etc.

MISSION — The Aardvark Dance Theatre will provide this city, state, and five state region with the highest quality modern ballet works created by contemporary American and European choreographers to a broad audience with special attention to young audiences.

OBJECTIVES —

Artistic: To develop a repertory with a wide range of contemporary ballet styles.

Performing: To expand and develop new dance audiences through regular home performance seasons.

Touring: To develop new dance audiences by bringing this dance program throughout the region at reasonable fees and ticket prices.

Management/personnel: To develop and maintain the management staff and systems necessary to achieve the above stated goals and objectives.

GLOSSARY

ACTION PLAN — an outline of the procedure used to implement a strategy and achieve a long-term goal. Thus, the action plan depicts the method by which a long-term goal and its associated strategy is converted into the short- and/or intermediate-term operating plans.

ACTORS' EQUITY ASSOCIATION (AEA) — the Craft Union which represents professional actors and stage managers in the United States. AEA has collective bargaining agreements with several associations of producing organizations including the League of Resident Theatres (LORT), the League of American Theatres and Producers, etc. The LORT contract has different provisions for different sized theatres, based on seating capacity and potential box office gross. LORT A is the largest, and LORT D the smallest. Developing (embryonic) companies can negotiate a "Letter Of Agreement" (LOA) directly with AEA.

BUDGET — a collection of numbers, organized into categories, which express the organization's priorities. A budget is a projection of expenses and income for defined activities, over a defined time period.

CONTRIBUTED INCOME — money given to the not-for-profit organization for which the donor receives no tangible exchange of goods or services. Contributions come from individuals, corporations, foundations, and the public sector (Federal, State, and local governments). Some managers use the term, "Unearned Income" to refer to contributions. Since this term has a very different meaning in the language of accountants, it is recommended that "Contributions" be used instead. See also, "Earned Income."

COSTED OUT — when the plan is "costed out," dollar values are attached to the various components. The result will be a budget.

DEFERRAL (OF PLAN) — putting off the implementation phase, usually due to an unforeseen change in the base circumstances.

EARNED INCOME — income to a not-for-profit organization resulting from an exchange of goods or services. Examples are income from ticket sales for shows which have already occurred, concessions income, and fees paid for performances on tour. See also, "Contributed Income."

EVALUATION — phase of planning where the organization determines how "successful" the plan has been. "Success" must be defined before the plan is implemented for the plan to be evaluated on a reasonable basis. An organization which doesn't know what its goals are, will have difficulty in achieving them.

EXTERNAL FACTORS — those factors over which the organization has no control. Examples include the economy (local and national), societal or local demographic changes, the weather, the competition, political structures, and tax or legal restraints.

FLESHING OUT — you "flesh out" a plan by adding detail to the outline — "meat on the bones."

FTE/FULL TIME EQUIVALENTS — jargon which describes numerically the people needed to accomplish something. These "people-numbers" can be added, subtracted, and otherwise manipulated in a budget. The formulas used to define FTE's vary from profession to profession. In the performing arts, convenient descriptions include man/hours, work weeks, half-time positions, volunteer hours, etc.

GOAL — a desired and obtainable result, such as a percentage or numerical increase in ticket sales or a dollar amount in contributions. One or more goals must be achieved to fulfill an objective (see "Objective").

IMPLEMENTATION — carrying out the plan, making strategic adjustments based on changing circumstances.

INTERNAL FACTORS — those factors which the organization can control. Examples include the marketing, finances, artistic product, advocacy efforts, and responses to external factors.

LORT B, LORT D, LOA (LETTER OF AGREEMENT) — see Actors' Equity Association (AEA).

MISSION — describes the basic activity or purpose of the organization, to include the "image" the organization wishes to project within the industry and professional community.

NET CURRENT ASSET POSITION — Barbara Hauptman uses this phrase to describe a situation where her not-for-profit organization has more easy-to-cash assets than obligations coming due at the end of the year. This is the result if the organization has been able to generate a surplus of income over expenses — a not-for-profit "profit"!

OBJECTIVE — the purpose to be achieved by an activity or sequence of related actions. An example of an objective may be, "to bring the organization into a broader spectrum of the community." Strategies — activities related to this objective — could include in-school programming, after performance discussions, touring to suburban communities, etc.
   GOALS and OBJECTIVES are sometimes used as interchangeable terms. FEDAPT makes a clear distinction between these two terms, based on the football analogy. The *objective* is to win the game. On the way to that objective, the team must achieve several *goals*. The STRATEGY outlines the approach the team expects to use to achieve the goals (short-term strategy) or objectives (long-term strategy).

STRATEGY — the effort undertaken to achieve an objective. This represents the way in which the organization's resources can be used to pursue the opportunities identified in the objective, while avoiding potential threats to the achievement of that objective.

STRATEGIC DIRECTION — the general, long-range "paths" which generally describe the direction in which an organizatin is moving. They are policies or broad guides to action which define the general parameters within which specific strategic objectives will be determined.

STRATEGIC PLANNING — FEDAPT uses the term, "Strategic Planning," to identify the process of planning strategy — of determining the step by step procedure to accomplish a goal. Thus, "Strategic Planning" is one part of "Long-Range Planning," "Institutional Planning," or just plain "Planning."
   The jargon varies considerably from field to field. In some businesses, for example, "Strategic Planning" means maximizing income through

careful positioning in the marketplace. Therefore, when utilizing the skills of a planning executive from the for-profit sector, it is important to begin by agreeing on the definition of terms.

SUCCESS — success is in the eye of the beholder, to borrow an old cliche. In planning, "success" must be defined before the plan is implemented. It may be defined as the achievement of all goals for the period, or as achieving a certain number of related goals, or in less specific terms, as some pre-defined movement in a specific strategic direction. In any case, "success" is defined early in the planning process, and referred to at the end of the implementation of that plan to determine whether the organization got to where it wanted to go.

UNEARNED INCOME — see "Contributed Income." In accrual accounting, "Unearned Income" is money received for services which have not yet been rendered. An example is subscription sales income before the first performance has opened, or advance sales ticket sales income.